CW00840094

OPTIMIZE FOR OUTCOMES

BETTER OUTCOMES FOR BETTER BUSINESS

Copyright

Optimize for Outcomes

First published in the United States of America

Address PO Box 1133, Sumner, WA, 98390, USA

ISBN 979-8644-590-292

Book cover design: Gina Sabini-Roberts & Sammie Covington

Editing: Greg Fidgeon

Dedication

This book – and the knowledge that it took to produce – would not be a thing if it weren't for all the people I've met along my life journey.

From Leslie, one of my first bosses when I was in high school working at a sporting goods store; to Scott, who gave me my first "technical" role at a tiny software company near Seattle; to Joel, who brought me in to structure a new team for a consulting company; and everyone in between. It is because of each and every one of you I had the pleasure of working with or for that I was able to write this book.

To everyone I've been able to help and to everyone who's been able to help me on our journeys of optimizing, this book is dedicated to you.

CONTENTS

Acknowledgements   x

Introduction   xii

    How to Get the Most out of This Book   xiv

    Keep In Touch   xiv

PART I   I

Laying The Foundation   I

Chapter I   2

Systems Thinking   2

    Defining Systems Thinking   2

    Effectiveness, Efficiency, and Productivity   3

        Examples From Heating Systems   4

    Relationship of Effectiveness, Efficiency, and Productivity   6

    To Summarize: 7

Chapter 2   8

Outcomes and Ultimate Outcomes   8

    Outputs vs. Outcomes   9

    Outputs Don't Guarantee Success   10

    Ultimate Outcomes   11

    To Summarize: 13

    Activity   13

PART II   14

Putting Your Business Into A Systems Thinking Framework   14

Chapter 3   15

Segmenting Your Business Into Systems   15

    The Five Pillars   16

    The Sales Cycle   16

    The Product Cycle   18

    Operations   19

    People Management   22

Culture   24

Systems In Your Business   25

To Summarize: 26

Activity   27

Chapter 4   28

Key Attributes of Systems   28

Inputs   28

Process Steps   29

Outputs   29

Metrics   30

Desired Outcomes   32

To Summarize: 33

Chapter 5   35

Relationship Between Attributes   35

Inputs, Process Steps, and Outputs   35

Outcomes and Metrics   37

What Does It All Mean?   37

An Example in Birthday Parties   38

Back to Business   40

To Summarize: 40

PART III   42

Improving Your Business   42

Chapter 6   43

Ensuring Alignment   43

Outcome Alignment and a Customer Journey   44

Alignment Within the System   45

Building a New System   47

Viewing Alignment with Different Lenses   47

To Summarize: 48

Chapter 7   49

Identify the System with the Most Opportunity   49

Pain Caused by Not Getting Outcomes   50

Effort to Fix or Resolve Issues   51

Impact if You Don't Remove the Pain   52

Operational Time Invested and Proportion of Revenue   53

Other Points to Consider   54

The Impact Prioritization Tool   55

To Summarize: 55

Activity   56

Chapter 8   57

Optimizing Your Systems   57

Effectiveness, Efficiency, or a Productivity Problem?   58

First, Eliminate   59

Next, Consolidate   61

Last, Automate   62

Coming Back to Productivity   64

To Summarize: 65

Chapter 9   66

Managing Change   66

When to Start Managing Change   66

After the Change   68

Metrics and Monitoring   69

When and What to Measure   71

Point-in-Time Versus Ongoing Metrics   72

Ongoing Metrics   73

To Summarize: 74

Chapter 10   75

Continuously Improve Where It Matters   75

Continuous Improvement is Continuous   75

Final Thoughts   76

Bonus Chapter 1   78

Root Cause Analysis and the Five Whys   78

Bonus Chapter 2   81

Using Swimlane Diagrams to Document a Process or System   81

What To Do Now?   84

    For the Brand-new Entrepreneur   84

    For the Established Business   85

    Specific System Problem Resolution   86

Case Study 1   89

The Small Company Looking to Scale   89

    Identifying Systems and Desired Outcomes   89

    Gathering Data for Analysis   91

    Making Changes   93

    Client Onboarding   94

    Developing Scalable Products   96

    Managing Change   97

Case Study 2   99

The Solo Entrepreneur Working To Build His New Business   99

    Start at the End   99

    Defining Needed Systems   100

    Thinking Through Product Development   101

    Change Management Light   102

Case Study 3   103

The Large Corporation   103

    Defining System Scope   103

    Adjusting the Approach   104

    Working Backward to Go Forward   105

    Documenting with Tools   107

    Outcome Alignment   108

    Using Tools to Improve   109

    Recommendations and Changes   110

    Final Results   112

Case Study 4   113

The Manufacturer   113
    Focusing Straightaway on a Specific System   113
    How to Get the Inputs   114
    Bringing it All Together   116
Glossary   117

ACKNOWLEDGEMENTS

First and foremost, I'd like to thank my wife, Brianna, for her undying support in anything and everything I do. This book would not have been possible without her in so many ways.

Colette Mason has been instrumental in getting this book to light. From her book writing guides to the "full Gordon Ramsey" motivation (as she likes to call it), her guidance and support were critical in getting this project completed.

Dan Meredith has been a good friend and mentor who has been through this journey with me, helping me to redefine my experiences from a corporate setting and build a way of thinking that applies to any business, regardless of size, and especially helpful to the small business entrepreneur.

Dexter Abraham was key to getting me out of my comfort zone. He was the first to challenge me to put what I do down on paper to teach others how to do the same. After I told him it couldn't be done, he told me to shut up and do it, and here we are.

I also want to acknowledge the businesses I've worked for and with over my career. Some of them provided the training and others the projects and environments to develop the methods taught in this book. Without those experiences, none of this would be.

Lastly, I want to thank my beta readers – Charles Hood, Adam Bresson, Rachel Jones, Shari Teigman and Fran Bradley – who helped me make sure that the material in the book makes sense to the average person and not just systems and process nerds like me.

INTRODUCTION

Hi. I'm Brian. Thank you for being interested in this book and optimizing your business to get better outcomes. I have a passion for helping others succeed in business. I wrote this book to take the mental models and tools I have learned and developed over 20 years of helping teams and businesses get better outcomes through process optimization. As I share these with you, you'll gain a better understanding of how to apply tools and techniques to your business to improve your outcomes too.

Early in my career, I found myself working in a consulting role where I was routinely put in front of Clients of all shapes and sizes and all different industries. One week, it would be a 100-person manufacturing company building hammers and screwdrivers. The next week, I'd be working with a Fortune 10 financial institution, and the next a 2,000-person firm in the retail food space. And on and on. Every week was a different company and a different challenge where I had to jump in and quickly add value by optimizing systems and processes.

To be effective, I needed to be able to quickly establish common ground. How could I go into a giant bank one week and help them solve their problems and then go into a 20-person nonprofit the next week and help them just as effectively? What I developed in short order was a mental model to make all these companies the same. It didn't matter how big they were or what they sold. It didn't matter what their business models were or where they sold. I could look at any company and 80 percent of it would be exactly the same as any other.

By thinking of companies in the same way, regardless of industry or business model, I could draw on previous experience and knowledge to help them without having to spend weeks or months digging deep into the details of each business. I developed a standard model, tools, and methods to be able to optimize and improve any company based on similarities of business characteristics, processes, and systems thinking.

Using these mental models, I could get dropped into any company on a Monday and be adding value to their business by Tuesday. By the end of the week, whatever company I am in will have accepted me as an expert in their field even though I didn't know much about their industry.

Once I had the initial mental model in place (which I now refer to as the Outcome Optimization Framework), I focused on learning how to improve processes. This included learning on the job from things I was doing and seeing, as well as formal training such as the Six Sigma Black Belt program I completed with one of my employers. I studied Lean, Kaizen, TQM (Total Quality Management), project management, and anything else I thought could apply to improve businesses.

This book represents the culmination of several months of working with small businesses and entrepreneurs to reformulate my mental models in a way that anyone can understand and apply to their own business, regardless of size, industry, or business model. In corporate environments, I have used these models to save and make companies hundreds of millions of dollars over 20 years. I have also helped individuals start new businesses, helped companies cut costs by 20 percent, scaled businesses to 3 times their revenue over 12 months, and much more.

You can benefit just the same by reading this book and applying what you learn to your business.

This book will help you understand why outcomes matter and how to streamline your operation to maximize the outcomes in your business. Whether you want to reduce costs, grow your revenue or build a large team, the information in this book will allow you to do so efficiently and effectively. You'll be able to Optimize for Outcomes yourself, leading you to the outcomes needed for long-term profitability and success.

One other quick note – I capitalize the words Customer and Client. This comes from my time spent working at Amazon, where Customer is treated as a proper noun. I've continued that tradition even after leaving Amazon because I still prioritize the Customer as the most important aspect of my business.

HOW TO GET THE MOST OUT OF THIS BOOK

EACH chapter builds on the previous information, so be sure you understand what you have read before moving on, otherwise you will struggle when it comes to the latter chapters.

At the end of Chapters Two, Three and Seven, there are activities that involve using one of my tools and applying the information from that chapter to your business. Whether your business is brand new or has been around for a while, you should complete the activities before moving on to the next chapter.

I regularly put out new tips, tricks, and tools through our mailing list. To sign up, visit our website at resources.optimizeforoutcomes.com and create an account. By doing so, you'll get access to all our tools and templates library at no cost to you.

KEEP IN TOUCH

If you have any questions, comments, or concerns, you can get in contact with me direct via brian@optimizeforoutcomes.com.

Find me on my Facebook page at https://www.facebook.com/OptimizeForOutcomes/

Thanks again for your interest in this book and let's get started helping you Optimize for Outcomes.

PART I
Laying The Foundation

"YOU CAN'T BUILD A GREAT BUILDING ON A WEAK FOUNDATION. YOU MUST HAVE A SOLID FOUNDATION IF YOU'RE GOING TO HAVE A STRONG SUPERSTRUCTURE."
GORDON B. HINCKLEY

CHAPTER 1

SYSTEMS THINKING

THE foundation of this book is a basic understanding of systems thinking and some related key terms. In turn, they will serve as the foundation for all your optimization and improvement efforts in your business. In this first chapter, we will cover:

- Systems thinking.
- Effectiveness, efficiency, and productivity.
- Real-world understanding/examples of these three elements.
- The relationship that the three elements have to each other.

DEFINING SYSTEMS THINKING

To properly define systems thinking, let's consider each word one at a time. "Thinking" is as it sounds and there's no special meaning associated other than defining your thoughts and how you process information. So far, so simple.

But the word "system" is a little bit different. System has many meanings and they can differ from person to person. Many think of software when they hear the word system, but this definition is too narrow for defining the term systems thinking.

In systems thinking, "system" refers to a combination of people, processes, and technology used to accomplish a task. A system can be 100 percent manual and not include any software at all. For example, if I ran a small business that sent out paper newsletters to physical addresses, I might have a system for printing those letters, folding them, putting them in an envelope, addressing those envelopes, and mailing them out through the post. The process of taking the letters off the printer, folding them, and getting them to the post office is performed by people. Just because it's not software doesn't mean it's not a system.

In your business, you may have systems for onboarding new Customers, for creating social media content, for converting leads into sales, and many other activities that you do regularly. The more you think of all the tasks you do as systems, the better you can take the information in this book and apply it to different areas of your business to make improvements. If you limit yourself to thinking of systems as software only, you will greatly reduce your ability to apply these principles and optimize your business for better outcomes.

> **"System" Definition**
>
> If you currently use this word to refer to software, try instead using "software", "application", or "app". It can also be helpful to think of your systems as the "activities" that you and your business perform every day.

EFFECTIVENESS, EFFICIENCY, AND PRODUCTIVITY

It is also vital that you understand these three terms – effectiveness, efficiency, and productivity – so you can maximize your optimization efforts. These terms are often confused with one another, used interchangeably, and are not used consistently by many people. But you must understand what these words mean to me and how they are used in the mental models and framework in the chapters ahead to get the most out of this book.

Effectiveness identifies how well a system output meets the needs of the Customer. Another way to think of effectiveness is that it measures how well a product or service solves a Customer's problem. For example, a home security system that doesn't go off when someone opens the front door isn't very effective. Its intended purpose of alerting the building's occupants when someone comes in the door is not being met, and the alarm system isn't going to give the Customer the outcome that he or she is seeking.

Effectiveness can be enhanced by improving your understanding of your Customer's needs/wants and better aligning your systems to produce outputs that align with your defined outcomes and better meet the needs of your Customers.

Efficiency is measured by the number of inputs (time, energy, money, etc.) that are used by your system to produce a given number of outputs. For example, assume a factory is producing 1,000 widgets a day (outputs/productivity) and uses 1,000lbs of steel (inputs). The efficiency of the factory is a ratio between the amount of steel used to the number of widgets produced.

Efficiency can be increased in three ways:

- Reducing the number of inputs and creating the same number of outputs (1,000 widgets with 800 pounds of steel).
- Using the same inputs and creating additional outputs (1,200 widgets with 1,000lbs of steel).
- Producing the same amount of outputs with the same amount of inputs, but in less time.

Productivity is a measure of outputs from your system. In other words, how much your system creates (outputs, value) in any given period. As an example, if you are working as a travel agent, your productivity for your work could be measured in how many trips you book in a day.

Productivity can increase by adding more inputs into the system which will, in turn, create more outputs. It can also be increased by becoming more efficient (easier said than done!).

EXAMPLES FROM HEATING SYSTEMS

Here's a real-world illustration of the differences between productivity, efficiency, and effectiveness: I have two fireplaces in my house, along with a furnace. One of the fireplaces is wood burning, while the other runs on natural gas. The furnace also runs on natural gas.

In producing heat for my home, I could build the biggest fire and generate the most heat with the wood-burning fireplace. The productivity of the wood fireplace is greater than both the gas fireplace and the furnace. But this productivity comes at a pretty heavy cost because I have to cut/store massive amounts of wood, use the wood to build a big fire, and keep feeding the fire to keep it going and to keep the productivity high (high outputs, but the process requires significant inputs).

The gas fireplace is much more efficient. It creates a smaller flame, but the flame generates a noticeable amount of heat. It's also fed from a gas line, which requires me to do nothing other than flip a switch. It cannot be as productive as the wood fireplace (generate as much heat), but the heat that it does generate comes at a fraction of the cost and none of the effort, making it much more efficient (lower outputs, but significantly lower inputs).

However, neither of these fireplaces is effective at heating the whole house. Only the furnace, with its extended, insulated ductwork, can heat the whole house effectively (outputs that meet the requirements of heating the whole house). If my desired outcome was to heat the whole house, the furnace would be my clear choice.

Note that effectiveness is partially determined by the lens you are using to view the situation. The gas fireplace is ineffective at heating the whole house, but very effective at heating the room it is in. Another lens to consider is that the fireplaces are very effective at controlling the climate in my house in a colder climate, but what if I lived in the tropics? My fireplaces wouldn't be any less productive because I can still generate the same amount of heat (outputs). But those outputs are the wrong outputs needed when it's 100 degrees outside. It's just not effective at controlling the climate in the right way.

In conclusion: the wood fireplace is the most productive, the furnace is the most effective (if my desired outcome is to heat the entire house), and the gas fireplace is the most efficient.

RELATIONSHIP OF EFFECTIVENESS, EFFICIENCY, AND PRODUCTIVITY

While these three concepts have relationships with each other, it is important to understand that success in one area does not guarantee success in all areas.

For example, becoming more efficient can make you more productive, but being more productive doesn't necessarily mean you are efficient.

Also, becoming more efficient does not guarantee you will be more productive. Think about this: If it takes me three hours to publish an article and I improve that to write the same quality and size article in two hours but spend the extra hour playing video games, I have gotten more efficient at writing articles but my productivity has not gone up.

People often believe they don't need to work on their efficiency as they're already super-productive. That's a mistake. This belief that productivity equals efficiency leads people to overlook things they could be improving. Even if you are highly productive, working on efficiency can help you:

- Be as productive as you are now with less effort.
- Be more productive than you are now with the same effort.

You do not have to be efficient or highly productive to be effective. You can meet your Customer's needs perfectly while being largely inefficient with systems that produce very little. But the downside here is the number of Customers you can serve will be very low until you increase efficiency and/or productivity.

And becoming more effective does not make you more efficient or productive. Great organizations are improving all three of these areas to stay ahead of the competition, maximize value to Customers, and maintain an agile organization that will be adaptable in the future.

TO SUMMARIZE:

- A system is a collection of people, processes, and/or technology designed to complete an activity.
- A system can be 100 percent automated with no people, 100 percent manual with no technology, or anywhere in between.
- Your business is a collection of systems, even if you don't think about it like that today.
- Productivity is a measure of your system outputs.
- Efficiency is the ratio of your system inputs to outputs.
- Effectiveness is a measure of how well the outputs of a system meet the intended purpose of said outputs.
- Being productive does not make you efficient or effective.
- Being efficient does not make you productive or effective.
- Being effective does not make you productive or efficient.

CHAPTER 2

OUTCOMES AND ULTIMATE OUTCOMES

EVERYTHING we do is because we desire an outcome. This is true as Customers and this is true as managers and business owners. We run ads and do marketing because we want leads. We want leads so we can make sales. We want sales so we can grow our business. We want to grow our business because we want money, we want to help people, or we want more freedom.

We brush our teeth because we don't want our teeth to fall out. We do laundry so we don't smell bad and offend the people around us.

Identifying the outcome you want from something is usually as easy as answering why you do what you do or why you want certain outputs from your system. Every system has one or more desired outcomes. We refer to them as "desired" because any system may or may not perform the way you expect and the outcomes you might get out of the system may not be what you want.

In this chapter, we'll cover the following topics:

- Understanding outputs vs. outcomes and why it matters.
- Outputs don't guarantee success.
- Ultimate outcomes.

OUTPUTS VS. OUTCOMES

It's important you do not confuse outputs with outcomes. The outputs are what you create from a system, but the outcomes answer the question as to why you want those outputs.

Outputs are the direct product of your processes and systems. For example, if you sell a course on how to improve a business's Facebook ads, one output you would have is the number of courses sold. While this is something you want to know and understand, it's less important than understanding the outcomes.

Outcomes are the results that come from getting the outputs. Another way to say it is that outcomes answer the question: "Why does getting these outputs matter?"

If you're selling courses on Facebook ads, this means understanding how you've helped people to improve their businesses. What are you trying to achieve with your course? You might answer this with something along the lines of: "I am helping business owners transform their ads from an annoying expense to a fountain of revenue."

A key reason this matters is because outputs by themselves will not create the results you're looking for most of the time. "Sales" is an output, whereas "closing on new business in a way that builds trust with my Customers and sets them up for success with their new product" is an outcome. If you are overly focused on the outputs, your outcomes won't get any better.

Outputs closely align with the concept of productivity while outcomes closely align with effectiveness. It is possible to be highly productive but completely ineffective in what you and your business are doing. Have you ever worked tirelessly for weeks or months on a project only to have it not do what you hoped? You put in hundreds of hours of work and were very productive, but you were not effective. If you only focus on outputs, you could spend many hundreds more hours but still not improve your outcomes at all.

Back to the example of selling the course on Facebook ads. Would you rather sell 100 courses that ended up doing nothing of value for your Customers or would you rather sell 80 courses that completely transformed the way your Customers run ads and get new business? Which one would be better for your business long term?

Ultimately, anything we do is for the outcomes. The outputs are a means to an end. Why do you have a business? It's not because you love running systems or because you enjoy doing accounting or delivering products/services. You want money, freedom, and personal fulfillment that comes with running a healthy, profitable business. You don't want to hire and fire people and you certainly don't want to deal with unhappy Customers, but these are all things you must do to get the outcomes that you want.

OUTPUTS DON'T GUARANTEE SUCCESS

Getting a perfect output doesn't always give you the outcomes your business needs. In fact, you can get many outputs right and still end up with poor outcomes. You could build the perfect course and have the perfect lead generation and sales systems that sell thousands, but if your delivery is poor and your Customers can't get through the course in a way that helps them improve their business, your mostly perfect outputs will not sustain your business long term.

It is helpful to understand your outputs, measure them, and improve them, but only when done looking at the greater context of outcomes.

An output focus is also a "build it and they will come" mentality. But if you build the wrong thing, nobody will come.

You can waste time over-optimizing outputs that don't give you better outcomes. If you focus on getting more and more sales but don't improve your delivery system and your Customers' ability to absorb and use the information you're teaching, you are over-optimizing your output and not getting better outcomes. The opposite is also true. You could spend too much time over-optimizing your course delivery system but that won't help you get better outcomes if you don't have sales.

With a focus on outputs, you run the risk of tricking yourself that you're being highly productive and successful even though your business is close to failing. If you focus on the output of sales and see some sales coming in, that's great – but it could give you a false sense of security. You might have sales today, but if you're not getting the right outcomes then they will disappear tomorrow. You will see yourself as productive but you really need to be effective. There are many examples of companies that have millions in sales but fail anyway because their outputs don't always translate to the outcomes needed for long-term success.

> **Outputs vs. Outcomes**
>
> Can you identify some companies that have gained the outputs (sales) but are no longer in business?

Focusing on outputs alone can lead to many hours sunk into your business that don't improve your outcomes. This will lead to frustration and self-doubt, questioning your ability to make your business work.

ULTIMATE OUTCOMES

Outcomes from one system often feed into the next system in your business. For example, you might have a system for driving traffic to a website that includes creating and running ads, a lead magnet, and the landing page.

The defined outcome of the system would be to generate qualified leads that are ready to buy your product. Those qualified leads then become the input into your next system of converting qualified leads into sales. The sales conversion system includes additional sales copy, additional testimonials, a trial version of your product, and additional giveaways. The desired outcome of that system is to generate accurate payments and happy new Customers that are using the products and getting value immediately.

Accurate payments are an input into a financial system and happy new Customers are an input into your ongoing Customer management system. And so on.

Eventually, you will reach what I call your ultimate outcome. This is the ultimate reason that you work, run a business, improve yourself professionally, etc. Researching thousands of answers to the question "why do you do what you do?", I can tell you there are three ultimate outcomes that everything ties back to for everyone:

- Money.
- Time/freedom.
- Personal fulfillment.

Many answers to the question involve two or three of these ultimate outcomes but they all fit into at least one of these three buckets. Some people want to travel the world, which takes time and money. Others want to volunteer at their favorite charity, which takes time and gives personal fulfillment. Some just want money and that's OK too (no judgment here). But everything you're doing will eventually lead to one of those three things.

These ultimate outcomes are also interrelated. Money can buy you time/freedom and personal fulfillment. You might use your money to pay for a housekeeper or food delivery. In any situation where you're paying someone to do work you would otherwise have to do then you're buying time with your money. You can also donate to charity, or spend your cash helping others or funding initiatives that you care about, which brings personal fulfillment. Freedom can also bring personal fulfillment if you use your free time to do things that are important to you.

When thinking about your desired ultimate outcomes, be honest with yourself. These will serve as a guiding light for everything you optimize. If you aren't true to what your desired ultimate outcome is, you will be aligning things to the wrong outcomes and wasting time, energy, and money. The better you can define these desired outcomes, the better you will be able to optimize.

TO SUMMARIZE:

- Everything we do, we do because we have a desired outcome from that activity or system.
- The outputs of a system answer the question "what?" while outcomes answer the question "why?".
- Understanding desired outcomes in turn helps you understand the effectiveness of your systems.
- These desired outcomes also serve as a "North Star" for everything you're doing to help you focus on making your systems more efficient and more productive.
- Ultimate outcomes are the fundamental reasons you do what you do – money, time/freedom, personal fulfillment.

ACTIVITY

Visit resources.optimizeforoutcomes.com and look for the Optimize For Outcomes Workbook. This workbook contains all the exercises from this book and can be downloaded free of charge.

Start with the Ultimate Outcomes Worksheet and complete the first half. You will complete the second half after Chapter 3.

PART II

Putting Your Business Into A Systems Thinking Framework

"YOU DON'T HAVE TO BE A GENIUS OR A VISIONARY OR EVEN A COLLEGE GRADUATE TO BE SUCCESSFUL. YOU JUST NEED A FRAMEWORK AND A DREAM"

MICHAEL DELL, DELL COMPUTERS

Chapter 3

SEGMENTING YOUR BUSINESS INTO SYSTEMS

IN my career, I've consulted with single-person start-up companies, Fortune 10 companies, and everything in between. I have spent time as a full-time employee of one of the largest, most valuable companies on the planet. I've also worked as an employee of a ten-person software business that made drivers for optical drives in the early 2000s.

So, I've seen hundreds of companies and how they work. And while we often focus on what makes us or our business unique, I'd say every one of these companies is 80 to 90 percent the same.

When I worked as a field engineer, the only way I could be successful was to establish commonalities between different organizations because I often had no more than a couple of hours to understand their business, their problems, and how to help them scale, save money, or both. What I eventually came to learn is that systems thinking allows you to look at any company and see common threads between them.

This also allows you to use the same tools and techniques to make any company better – including yours.

As you start to think about segmenting your business into systems, you don't have to start from scratch because every business has the same core pillars and similar systems. You might not execute them the same way, you might have different desired outcomes, and some systems might be more important to you that aren't important to other businesses, but the pillars and systems are there whether you think about them this way today or not.

THE FIVE PILLARS

There are five core pillars to every business. Each company treats these pillars differently and puts different amounts of energy into developing them, but they are all there in every company.

They are:

- Sales Cycle.
- Product Cycle.
- Operations.
- People Management.
- Culture.

Let's take a look at each of these in more detail so you get a better understanding of their role and importance.

THE SALES CYCLE

Every business needs sales. This pillar includes systems for generating traffic, identifying qualified leads from the traffic, and converting those leads into sales.

A sales cycle exists whether you are a physical store, a reseller, only sell online, have physical products, sell digital products, or any combination of attributes. The sales cycle starts when you first contact a potential customer and ends when the sale is completed. You might have additional sales cycles (like selling other products to Customers that have already bought something from you) in your business.

Think about a car dealership. They have physical products and services sold to a relatively local market. They need to generate traffic, i.e. awareness that they exist and have products for sale. They might run ads in a local newspaper or on a radio station. They might target ads on social media to specific ZIP codes. They possibly have a billboard or two in the area surrounding the dealership. The creation and management of the ads fall within a traffic system that the dealership operates whether they think about it like this or not.

This traffic system generates traffic to their dealership but not everybody that visits the dealership is ready or able to buy a car. They will have a process to engage visitors, to understand where they're at in their car buying process, and to help them understand the cars and the purchase process. The dealership is also looking to qualify good leads by gauging visitors' interest in the vehicles, taking them for test drives, doing credit checks, etc. Eventually, the most qualified leads enter a sales closing system which includes negotiating a final price, securing financing if needed, and a stack of paperwork.

This is a simple, high-level example, but it illustrates the point of a sales cycle for a business that has physical products in a physical location.

A course creator selling digital products through a virtual store might have different mechanics but will have a very similar sales cycle. They will run ads through social media and online channels to generate traffic and awareness. This traffic goes through some sort of qualification, perhaps by downloading a lead magnet (showing more interest by being willing to give up an email address) or filling out the form to receive more information. These are just two examples and there are many ways to qualify traffic to leads when working online.

Those that do turn into qualified leads enter the course creator's sales closing system. This might include an email sequence that provides additional information to the potential Customer, testimonials from other Customers that have been successful with the course creator's products, or other sales copy that highlights the benefits of their products. Eventually, some of these qualified leads will turn into sales.

While some elements of these two companies are different, the system framework is identical. There is a traffic system, a lead qualification system, and a sales closing system that moves people from being unaware that a product or company exists through to completing the purchase with that company.

The traffic systems for both the dealership and the digital course creator have similar inputs, process steps, outputs, and desired outcomes. The traffic system inputs are advertisements, sales copy, people, etc. There are processes that get these people to view and understand the ad and drive interested parties to take action. The lead qualification system helps identify who is ready to buy and who is just window shopping. The sales closing system takes the qualified leads, adds additional information to help in a purchasing decision, and facilitates the exchange of contracts and money.

THE PRODUCT CYCLE

Every business has at least one product and that is a result of a product cycle. This includes systems to develop a new product, deliver it to Customers, and provide support for that product. It also includes feedback loops from various Customer experiences from other parts of the business and other systems.

In the automotive industry, new cars and new models are constantly being developed. Car manufacturers take input from a variety of sources to develop new features and models every year. Those cars eventually get delivered to Customers following purchases made in dealerships and mechanics provide ongoing support for those cars as the Customers use the product.

Meanwhile, our digital course creator has the same product cycle and systems. He or she develops a course on a particular topic through a product development system. Those courses live in a delivery system where Customers can access them. A support system helps Customers that are having trouble accessing or using the courses. The savvier course creators include a part of their support system that helps Customers use course information to get better outcomes themselves.

Again, you can see the elements differ, but the pillars and systems are the same for these two very different businesses.

OPERATIONS

Operations can be broken up into six subcategories that cover all the administrative tasks required to run a company. This includes technology, business intelligence, knowledge management, task and priority management, and process management.

Let's look at those individually.

TECHNOLOGY

Technology covers the hardware and software used by your business and can be further broken down into two main subgroups – acquisition and management.

How do you acquire technology? You need to figure out what you need, what your options are, and how you implement your technology.

For example, say you identify the need to implement a new Customer Relationship Management (CRM) application. How do you identify the requirements you have in your business for this new CRM? What specific needs do you have around functionality?

There are many options for CRMs today. How do you analyze these different options? Which one best meets your requirements? And once you've identified your chosen application; how do you go about implementing this new technology?

How do you manage the technology that you have? Once you've bought your new CRM, who will manage and take care of it and how? Who adds new users? Who turns on new features? How do you make sure the software you have continues to meet your business's needs?

BUSINESS INTELLIGENCE

Business intelligence is about how you capture, manage, and consume data about your Customers, partners, operations, employees, etc.

How do you capture data from the different areas in your business? Which systems have data that provide your business insights? What are the different tools in your business that have data in them that you could use for business intelligence purposes?

Just capturing data doesn't mean you have useful information. Data will come in different formats and from different sources. You'll have data from a website such as traffic metrics, data from a CRM application on Client contacts and sales, and data from your help system that supports Customers having trouble with your products, to name a few. How are you managing all this data and how are you bringing it together in a way that tells the right story?

Once you bring the data together, you still need to present it in a way that is consumable for the intended audience. Do you present this data in Microsoft Excel or Google Sheets? Do you use a purpose-built tool such as Power BI or Tableau? What types of dashboards do you create for those that need the data and information? How do you manage and update these dashboards?

KNOWLEDGE

More and more, business is becoming about managing knowledge and information. With technology like the internet and cell phones, we are constantly bombarded with information; some of it important and some of it not. What tools and processes do you have in place to manage knowledge in your business?

Are you using tools like Evernote or OneNote? Do you use SharePoint to manage documents? How do you manage links to relevant websites? How is knowledge shared across teams and individuals in your business? Do you share knowledge with partners or others who are external to your company?

TASK AND PRIORITY MANAGEMENT

As well as being bombarded with knowledge, we are also hit with things we need to do, things we should do, and things we want to do. What tools and processes are you using to manage your tasks and priorities?

There are too many things that need to be done for you to remember just in your head. If you don't keep track of your tasks elsewhere, you are bound to forget some things or let something slip through the gap. Using an application to help you manage your tasks will ensure you don't forget to do things that need to get done.

Priority management is critical in making sure you are doing the right things at the right time. It can be overwhelming to have a list of 100 items that need to be accomplished when they're not in any kind of order. If you don't know where you're supposed to begin, you can end up focusing on the wrong things or become overwhelmed to the point where you simply shut down and do nothing. With a prioritized list, you can focus on your number one task before moving on to number two.

It's important with priority management to have actual priorities and stack ranks. There should be a number one priority and that should be followed by a number two priority and so on. All too often, I see businesses that say that "everything is important". But when everything is a priority, nothing is a priority.

PROCESS MANAGEMENT

Processes are often overlooked or neglected, especially when a business is young. Processes are arguably the most valuable thing about your business. Your processes are how you create value for your Customers. Without your business processes, you can't create and deliver your products and you can't create the associated value for your Customers. No value equals no Customers.

How do you manage your processes? What is your documentation strategy? When you create process documents? Where do you store them? How do you manage them? When do you update them? These are all questions you want to answer as part of a process strategy.

While there is a lot here specific to operations, and it can seem over-whelming, it doesn't have to be overly complicated. You don't need to buy million-dollar tools to manage your processes.

Having a basic strategy to store information in Google Docs and record processes using process narratives – a story to define your processes and how they are performed – is a fine way for a company to manage its processes, especially if it's a smaller business.

Managing the knowledge of your business in a single OneNote notebook is perfectly fine, too. As your business grows, you might outgrow some of these simple methods to manage operations, but don't feel like you need fancy technology or complicated mental models and systems to get the job done.

ACCOUNTING

Accounting covers the system or systems used to record and manage incoming revenues and outgoing expenses. It might include an expense management application and other tools used to track money and financial transactions through your business.

Accounting systems can be simple. A spreadsheet keeping track of incoming and outgoing transactions is fine for starters. Additional financial software can be added as needed to quickly increase the sophistication of your accounting systems.

PEOPLE MANAGEMENT

There are four main areas of managing people – hire, rewire, inspire, and retire. Even if you're a company of one today, it's important to understand and plan for managing people in the future.

Note that many of the principles in managing people apply to managing contractors, virtual staff, or even freelancers that might help you in your business. From here on in this book, I will refer to all potential staff as employees.

HIRE

Finding the right people to help you in your business is one of your most important tasks. A good employee can greatly improve your business while a bad one can ruin everything you've worked hard to build.

But hiring the right people is not that easy and is not usually something you're taught in school. Your hiring system should include the following processes:

- How to identify a need for hiring.
- How to document the work in a job description or similar.
- How to find potential candidates for fulfilling the work.
- How to screen candidates to find the one you want.
- How to onboard new employees.

REWIRE

When new employees come on board, they need to be taught how your business does things and how to best fit in. They need to know your expectations, as well as how your systems function. Increasingly, employees also need continuous education to keep up with changes in technology and how those changes affect your business.

INSPIRE

Management and leadership are important skills when having employees of any kind. These should be developed by you and others that you have managing and leading in your company.

RETIRE

Retire is a word I used to describe multiple reasons employees might leave your company, all of which should be planned for. In this category, you should include:

- Voluntary departure management – when someone leaves their role based on their decision (actual retirement, moving to another company, or promotion to a new role).
- Involuntary departure management – when someone leaves their role based on the company's decision.

- Succession planning – planning for departures.
- Transition planning – moving an employee from one role to another.

CULTURE

Culture is often overlooked as something that requires proactive attention. Especially when companies are small, working on culture seems to be near the end of the priority list. But this can cause problems later as your company grows and can eventually undo your hard work.

Imagine a child raising himself in the forest with no guidance or parenting from other people. The child will continue to grow and form his own opinions about how the world should be and how things work. That child would likely have problems when placed in an environment with other people. It's not that the child doesn't develop or doesn't become an adult. Their development still happens but without good guidance and proactive effort, the outcome will most likely be undesirable.

Company culture is similar. If you ignore it, it will still develop on its own. However, it probably won't be what you wanted and nor will it be right for long-term success. I have seen companies fail because they ignored proactively developing their culture and ended up with a toxic environment that ultimately caused significant problems in maintaining a good business.

Company culture will determine how your employees think and act. It will influence how you and your employees make decisions. It will influence how hard your employees work – and that will influence how teams collaborate and how people get things finished (or don't).

Company culture is defined by a collection of artifacts, policies, history, and work practices. Artifacts include things like mission and vision statements, leadership principles, manifestos, and similar items that establish beliefs of the business.

These elements work together to give your employees an understanding of what is expected of them and how they can operate within the capacities of their roles. It will encourage them to take risks or discourage them from stepping up. It will influence their mindset and how they show up for work. Ultimately, culture will make or break your company.

Even if you are a solo entrepreneur, you would benefit from spending some time working on defining the culture you want in your business. It will help you better define how you want to operate and what things you want to prioritize. It will also be better to have these things in place before you start growing and adding new people to your business.

SYSTEMS IN YOUR BUSINESS

Whether you realize it or not, your business has systems. You might not think of them as such – or you may neglect them massively – but they are there, nonetheless.

Now, I don't mean to overwhelm you with all the things you are not currently thinking about in your business or all the systems you need in place to be successful. But they do need consideration.

Like the processes covered earlier in this chapter, your systems do not need to be overly complicated to function and serve your business well. A simple application or process is all that's needed for many of your systems to be good enough, particularly if your business, as it stands today, is smaller. Again, you can adjust as and when it grows.

Look at the framework below and use it as a guide to help you think about your business in systems and to start identifying where you have the biggest opportunities to improve what you're doing to get better outcomes for your business.

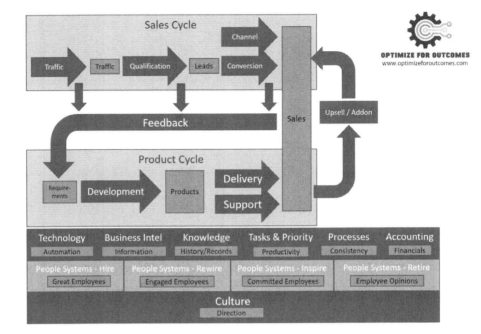

See this image in full color at https://www.optimizeforout-comes.com/wp-content/uploads/2020/05/Company-Systems.jpg

TO SUMMARIZE:

- All businesses, large and small across every industry, are 80 to 90 percent the same.
- Every business is built on Five Pillars (although some of the pillars might be more like tree stumps for a particular business):
  - Sales Cycle.
  - Product Cycle.
  - Operations.
  - People Management.
  - Culture.
- Your business exists on these pillars and has systems for these areas whether you think about it like this today or not.

ACTIVITY

Complete the second half of the Ultimate Outcomes Worksheet, reviewing your fundamental business systems.

You can use the Five Pillars Worksheet to inventory your systems across your business in greater details. (optional at this point)

You can find the Optimize For Outcomes workbook at resources.optimizeforoutcomes.com

Chapter 4

KEY ATTRIBUTES OF SYS-TEMS

NOW that you're more aware of the systems in your business, it is important for you to identify and understand the key attributes of each. We will talk about each of these attributes using an example of a core system of onboarding a new Customer.

In this chapter, we will cover:

- Inputs.
- Process Steps.
- Outputs.
- Metrics.
- Desired Outcomes.

INPUTS

Inputs are the pieces used by the system at the start of each step. Let's think about onboarding that new Customer. For our example, we'll also say that our business is a gym and that our Customer has purchased a personal training package in addition to signing up as a member.

The inputs needed to onboard this new Customer would include things like an information pack about gym hours and amenities, gym policies, the branded water bottle given to all new Customers, a calendar of availability for the first training sessions, and information about the training package. This is not meant to be an exhaustive list but includes some of the things you would expect to see as inputs into onboarding.

PROCESS STEPS

Process steps include everything your business does to complete the system of onboarding a new Customer. They define the order in which each step occurs and can include details on who performs each step.

In our gym, we might define our onboarding process to start immediately after payment is received from a new Client. Use a process narrative to write out the steps, such as:

1. Clear the payment through the credit card processing system.

2. Once cleared, provide the new Customer with their information pack and gym policies guide.

3. Highlight the gym hours and Customer service number in the information pack should they have any questions.

4. Bring up the personal training schedule and find a time that works for the Customer to have their first session.

5. Etc…

This narrative would continue until you have defined all the steps that complete this system.

OUTPUTS

Outputs, naturally, are the things that come out of your process steps as a result of going through the process. They are one of the fundamental reasons any business exists. All businesses take inputs and, through their process, creates outputs that are more valuable to the business's Customers than the inputs. Outputs are oftentimes connected to the value your Customers perceive that your business offers.

Back to our gym and our onboarding process, the most important output from this process is an educated new Customer. At the start of our onboarding process, they knew very little about how our gym operates and what they need to do to get the full value of the product they have just purchased.

Once a new Customer has gone through the onboarding process, they are now educated on when they can use the gym, who to contact for help and how to contact them, and they know how to schedule their personal training sessions and have the first session on the calendar. The scheduled session would be considered a second output of our onboarding process.

By moving this Customer through our onboarding process, we have added value to their world and moved them closer to reaching their fitness goals. It is by creating these more valuable outputs that our business generates revenue and happy Customers.

> **Core of Systems Thinking**
>
> Inputs go through process steps to create outputs. Outputs from one system become inputs to the next.
>
> For example, an output from your web traffic system could be leads that then become inputs into your sales conversion system.

METRICS

Every core system that you define should have at least one metric to help you understand the health of that system. A metric is a measurement or data point about the system and process it applies to. Simply, the metric is something that you can measure that will give you insights into how your system is performing. For example, a metric for the system you use to make sales is conversion percentage.

If you've ever been through training on goal setting, you're quite possibly familiar with the SMART acronym. The same acronym applies to how you define metrics for your core systems.

S – specific. This means that your metric is specific enough that nobody in your business is unsure as to what it means or what it's measuring. For example, if I defined a metric of "happiness", that's not very specific and could mean a lot of things. The happiness of employees? The happiness of Customers? Happiness when? To make this a more specific goal related to our example, I could define a metric of "happiness of our Customer after the onboarding process". There is no question of what I'm trying to measure and what that metric tells me.

The second part of Specific is to define what "good" is. There are different ways to do this depending on the properties of the metrics that you define. For example, let's give our Customer a five-question survey to measure their happiness after the onboarding process. Each question is a scale of one to ten with ten being the best. I could define "good" as a cumulative score of 45 points or higher with no single score lower than eight. Again, this is very specific and nobody should be confused about what I'm measuring and what's considered good or bad.

M - measurable. This means that I can measure the metric that I defined. If, for example, I said I was going to measure the level of endorphins in our Customer's body to see if they're happier after our onboarding process, this is not measurable in our gym. I can, however, measure Customer satisfaction with the onboarding process by having them complete that survey we mentioned above at the end of the process.

A - achievable. You should ensure the metrics you define are realistically achievable. If I defined a metric specific to how fast we scheduled our first training session with our Customer and said every session must happen within 24 hours of the Customer joining our gym, I'm going to be disappointed. Realistically, this is not an achievable metric because many will schedule their first session further out than 24 hours.

R - relevant. The metrics that you set should be relevant to the system you're trying to measure. For example, measuring a Customer's weight loss is a useful metric for understanding the effectiveness of your training programs but doesn't have anything to do with your onboarding system. Make sure the metrics that you define are specific to the system that you are analyzing.

T - timely. Make sure that the metrics you define are clearly defined at or for a specific time. We talked about this a little bit related to S or Specific. You don't want a metric identified just as "Customer happiness". Customer happiness when? Customer happiness for how long? Each metric should be associated with a point in time in your activity, such as Customer happiness after onboarding.

You could use a combination metrics specific to time too. Customer satisfaction before onboarding versus Customer satisfaction after onboarding, as an example. In any case, make sure any metrics you define are related to a specific time in your activity.

DESIRED OUTCOMES

Ultimately, anything we do in our business (and personal lives as well) we do because we are looking for specific outcomes. We talked earlier about outputs that define the "what". Outcomes define the "why".

Defining why you're doing something gives you a deeper understanding of your activities in your business. It is also entirely possible to get the right outputs but not get the outcomes from your business activities needed for long-term success. Companies can have millions of dollars in sales and still go out of business. Likewise, companies don't need perfect outputs to reach great outcomes (Can you make a better hamburger than the large fast food chains?). Defining your desired outcomes and aligning them across your systems will help you achieve greater long-term success.

In our gym example, we defined two important outputs of our onboarding process; an educated new Customer and a scheduled session for personal training. Why do we want these? Well, we want an educated new Customer so that they don't hurt themselves, have unrealistic expectations, and so they don't trash our gym. We want the first session scheduled because we know that only through putting in the work will the Customer see results, and getting that first session scheduled makes them more likely to do the work and more likely to get the results they are looking for to be happy with our service.

By having these defined desired outcomes, we can now make sure our core system has all the right ingredients. These outcomes can also help us define some of our metrics.

We said we wanted to make sure new Customers don't hurt themselves. Are we giving them the right information so they know how to use the equipment without injuring themselves? Do we need to change part of our process, provide safety training, or include additional support as part of their membership? Do we have a metric that tells us if we are achieving this outcome or not (we can measure how many of our Customers injure themselves in the gym)?

Now that everything is defined, we have a much better understanding of what we need out of our system and how we are doing today. This becomes the foundation for improvements to our business to either scale larger or improve our efficiency and reduce costs.

TO SUMMARIZE:

- Inputs are the resources a system uses to produce its outputs.
- Process Steps are what happens inside a system to get from start to finish.
- Outputs are the things that a system produces.
- Metrics are measurements that help you understand the health of your systems.

- Desired Outcomes answer the question: "Why do you want the good outputs of this system?"

Chapter 5

RELATIONSHIP BETWEEN AT-TRIBUTES

UNDERSTANDING the relationship between the attributes covered in previous chapters – inputs, process steps, outputs, metrics, etc. – will put you in a better place to optimize your business for better outcomes.

To help you along the way, in this chapter we'll go in-depth on the following topics:

- How inputs, process steps, and outputs are related.
- How outcomes are achieved from system outputs.
- How metrics help you understand the health of your system.

INPUTS, PROCESS STEPS, AND OUT-PUTS

In short, inputs are changed into outputs by process steps. Anything done by employees in a business will show this concept. Inputs are taken and processed in some way that creates outputs that are more valuable to a business than the inputs. This value might be created for paying Customers or could be value created specifically for the business.

An easy example of this is to think about a company that makes cars. The car manufacturer starts with inputs in the form of rubber, metal, glass, and electronics, among other things. These inputs get fed into the company's manufacturing process steps. Components are made and assembled, glass is installed, wheels are manufactured and added to what eventually becomes the output – the car. It's painted (paint is another input) and eventually shipped off to a car dealership to be sold.

The inputs, like rubber and sheet metal, aren't valuable to most people. But the car manufacturer can make them so by processing them into an output (a car) that is valuable to their Consumers.

INPUTS AND OUTPUTS FOR AN INTERNAL PROCESS

Some activities are internally focused and don't produce outputs that are purchased by Customers. This doesn't mean the activities are any different. In fact, they are quite similar in terms of inputs increasing in value through process steps that create outputs. In other words, the framework applies to systems that are internally focused (on helping you and employees of your business) just as it applies to paying Customers.

For example, any company bigger than a few people will have systems related to hiring staff. The activity of recruiting new employees has inputs, process steps, and outputs, just like making a car. Some of the inputs into a recruiting activity include the needs of the business, a job description, and benefits information.

There are process steps involved that include posting vacancies to job boards, processing incoming applications, interviewing qualified candidates, and making a hiring decision.

These process steps have outputs. An applicant goes through the process step of an initial screening phone call and turns into an output; a rejected candidate or a qualified candidate.

That qualified candidate is an input to the process step of an in-person interview. The in-person interview step hopefully produces the one candidate you want to hire as an output and so on until the person is hired and the end of the system is reached.

OUTCOMES AND METRICS

Outcomes are the results and impact you get from using your systems. Sometimes multiple systems influence or create a single outcome.

Thinking back to our car manufacturer, they might have the desired outcome of creating happy Customers who love their cars. While the car contributes to reaching this outcome, it's not the only ingredient. Other systems – including the sales process experience, the ability to get financing, and aftercare provided – also contribute to a Customer feeling happy about their purchase.

Any company can create outputs but only those that can define and achieve the right outcomes will be successful long term.

Metrics allow us to understand things like effectiveness, efficiency, and productivity of the things that we're doing to create the products we're making. They tell us how much steel is used to produce our car, how much steel is wasted in the process, and how to measure the quality of our car when it's finished. Metrics can tell us if our Customers are happy or dissatisfied by helping us to understand if we are reaching their desired outcomes. Without metrics, you will have no idea if you're doing the right things or if those things are sustainable, both critical to understanding how to be successful over time.

WHAT DOES IT ALL MEAN?

Knowing the relationships between the different key attributes helps you to understand how to fix problems in your business.

At the end of the day, all any business owner cares about is reaching their desired outcomes, whether that be money and time to help their favorite charity, spend more time with their family, or be able to buy the nice things that they desire.

If you're not getting the outcomes you desire, understanding this relationship between attributes will help you pinpoint the problems and make the corrections needed to improve your outcomes.

Ultimately, there is no other way to change your outcomes than to change the inputs and process steps of your core activities.

Tie this back to the definitions of productivity, efficiency, and effectiveness from Chapter One. As you move to better understand the role of systems in your business and how you need to optimize your systems for better outcomes, knowing where to focus becomes critical in making the right improvements.

Remember that productivity is a measure of outputs. If you find you need to increase productivity, understanding the relationship between the attributes will direct you to where you should focus your improvements and to what you should be doing.

Efficiency is a relationship between the inputs, process steps, and outputs. If you need to cut costs, becoming more efficient means improving the ratio of inputs to outputs or reducing process time.

And effectiveness is how well the outputs serve their intended purpose and how that helps you get the outcomes you're looking for. If you need to improve effectiveness, you'll need different outputs (or a different problem to solve).

AN EXAMPLE IN BIRTHDAY PARTIES

Let's try and tie this all together in one example. Imagine you are throwing a birthday party and the desired outcome is having the best party that any of the attendees have been to this year. What would you need to make this happen?

Everybody will define this slightly differently but for now let's say this means having good food, the right cake, some activity like swimming or karaoke, and the right people.

To make this happen, there is a system specific to getting the best food, there's a system specific to creating the right cake, there is a system specific to getting karaoke working, and there's a system in getting the right people to attend.

If we think about the system specific to making the cake, we can define the inputs. You'll need flour, sugar, spices, frosting, candles, etc. There is a process involved which includes things like mixing the dry ingredients, mixing the wet ingredients, mixing everything, greasing your pan, pouring the batter into the pan, baking the mixture, etc.

Each process step has inputs and outputs. The step of baking the cake has inputs of a greased pan and batter. The output is the baked cake. That baked cake is an input into our next step which is adding the frosting. Inputs into this next step include the baked cake and frosting while the output is a frosted cake.

A metric we would have that tells us if we did a good job or not is the happiness level of all our guests at the end of the party. If everyone's happiness level is high, then everything is great, and we don't need to do anything different next year.

But if we have some unhappy guests or marginally happy guests, we haven't reached our desired outcome. If we have no other metrics, we will be left to guess which part of the party they didn't like. While it's possible we could guess correctly, it's more likely we will guess wrong and not understand what we need to improve to make our party better.

If we had a few basic metrics such as how many people ate cake, how many people liked the cake, and what are the reasons people didn't eat cake, we could rule out or rule in the cake's contribution to us not reaching our desired outcomes.

Let's now assume we got the metrics and we can see half the people that ate the cake didn't like the flavor. We now have good insights into what to fix to make our next party better and to understand that the "effectiveness" of the cake is where we went wrong. To fix it, we go back to the inputs into the cake and make our changes there. We might use different spices next time, or more sugar. Maybe we forgot the eggs or put on too much frosting.

If we didn't establish that our cake was the ineffective factor, we'd be left guessing and quite possibly wasting time, energy, and money on fixing things that don't matter – or even make things worse.

It's possible there was no cake left at the end of our party and we assumed we need more cake (more productivity) next year.

But in reality, most of the cake ended up in the garbage because people didn't like the taste. We just didn't notice. So next year, we could go out and buy twice as much cake thinking that will solve the problem, but still disappoint people with the flavor. And we'd be in an even worse position than we were the year before because we are still getting the same outcome (people still don't like the flavor of the cake) but we spent twice as much money increasing our cake productivity.

BACK TO BUSINESS

Making improvements in your business works the same way. When you're not getting the outcomes that you want, you need to identify the systems and outputs that relate to that outcome, understand if you're trying to fix productivity, efficiency, or effectiveness, and then change the inputs and process steps within those systems.

Understanding how all these things relate will help you focus your time and energy on the right things that will help you Optimize for Outcomes.

TO SUMMARIZE:
- Inputs, through process steps, become outputs.
- The process steps add value to the inputs.
- Outcomes are created by one or more outputs.

- If you want different outcomes, you need to change your inputs and process steps.
- Metrics will help you make data-based decisions instead of guessing.

PART III

Improving Your Business

"IF YOU ALWAYS DO WHAT YOU'VE ALWAYS DONE,
YOU'LL ALWAYS GET WHAT YOU'VE ALWAYS GOT."
HENRY FORD

Chapter 6

ENSURING ALIGNMENT

FAILING to think of your business in separate systems and pieces can lead to actions that do not contribute positively to your overall goals and desired outcomes.

But acknowledging this failure allows you to correct it by ensuring an alignment between the desired outcomes of your systems and those of your business.

In this chapter, we'll cover the following concepts:

- Aligning system inputs, processes, and outputs to desired outcomes.
- Building new systems that are aligned from the start.
- Using different lenses to gain additional perspectives.

Each of your systems should have an identified desired outcome or outcomes. Defining these clearly for each system will make it easier for you to improve the system, troubleshoot, and ensure you and your team fully understand and are aligned with its purpose.

You can also ensure your desired outcomes are aligned with one another and not in conflict (and therefore preventing any from being achieved). Likewise, you can ensure each aligns with the ultimate outcome established for your business.

While this may seem a simple concept, this is where businesses often get confused and create problems for themselves. Systems are developed in isolation and can often contain inputs, steps, and/or outputs that don't contribute to you getting the business outcomes you want (or take you away from them). This extra effort is a waste and is one of the leading causes of inefficiency in your business.

OUTCOME ALIGNMENT AND A CUSTOMER JOURNEY

As an example, let's consider the Customer Journey at a restaurant. A Customer Journey defines the experience your Customer has when buying something from your business.

First, we identify the desired outcome overall. In this case, we will say this is a high-end restaurant that wants to make its Customers feel like royalty in its meal delivery.

We then start to identify the core activities that help us, as the restaurant, to deliver this experience. We have five different activities which include greeting and seating, pre-meal management, meal preparation, meal delivery and follow-up, and table closeout. Each of these activities combined creates the outcomes of our restaurant's Customer journey.

As we look at what we're doing as a restaurant business, we must ensure our desired outcomes of each of these activities are aligned with our desired outcome of maintaining a high-end restaurant that makes Customers feel like royalty. Conversely, we can use this desired outcome of our Customer journey to help us define the desired outcomes of each of our different activities.

Ask yourself, what would be the desired outcome of the greeting and seating element to ensure that Customers felt like royalty? We might define it as an initial Customer experience that sets a regal tone and delights our Customers through five-star treatment.

However, if our desired outcome for greeting and seating was defined as seating the Customer as quickly and economically as possible, our outcome for this activity is quite possibly out of alignment with our desired outcome of our Customer journey. Think about it. Rushing Customers to their table or providing self-seating would not generally make them feel like royalty, right?

Having defined outcomes specific to providing a royal greeting and seating experience, we must then ensure the process steps are aligned with the desired outcome of greeting and seating. We must make sure Customers coming in the door are greeted promptly, that we communicate to them how happy we were to be able to serve them today, and do things such as verifying reservations and offering to check their coats.

We would do the same analysis with each of our activities – defining our desired outcomes, ensuring those outcomes are aligned with our desired business outcomes, and then building a system to deliver what we have defined. As we go through this process, we also want to ensure that any outcomes we've defined for our systems align with the defined outcomes of the other systems.

ALIGNMENT WITHIN THE SYSTEM

Do you remember the relationship between the attributes of a system? Inputs go through process steps to create outputs and those outputs, in turn, create outcomes. Once you have a system with well-defined desired outcomes that align with the outcomes of the broader business, you can start to align the individual attributes to the desired outcomes of the system.

Thinking about our restaurant and its greeting and seating system, we can consider what we're doing as a business and how it aligns with our desired outcome of setting a regal tone and delighting our Customers through five-star treatment.

We can identify outputs that we need to create this experience for our Customers. We will need the Customers to be seated at their table and may want them to have menus in hand as quickly as possible. We want to ensure the table is already prepped and ready to go. This might include having fresh, hot bread arrive at the table seconds before the Customers are seated.

We can also identify the inputs we need and the process steps we will take to move through our system from start to finish. We will need menus, fresh hot bread, silverware, napkins, etc. as inputs to our greeting and seating system. We will need to move Customers from the front door greeting area to their designated table. We might need to provide additional information on daily specials or new items on our menu. We might pull out/push in the chairs as Customers sit down. We also might help them with their napkins since they are royalty in our restaurant.

You also want to ensure that your inputs align with your outputs. As the saying goes: "Garbage in, garbage out." This is true of any of your business systems as well. You are not going to be able to create a royal meal with subpar ingredients. Likewise, the opposite is true. If you are running a restaurant with the desired outcome of providing the most cost-effective dinners for families, you cannot load your meals with expensive, super high-quality ingredients.

If you are analyzing an existing system, this is an opportunity to identify wasteful inputs and process steps to eliminate or reduce.

As an example, we might identify that current place settings at the table include nine pieces of silverware that need prepping for each Customer, but we might realize that we can use five pieces and still preserve our regal experience. Reducing the silverware will lead to less prep time and less time doing dishes later.

This is also an opportunity to identify inputs or process steps that are missing in the systems. Perhaps you realize you were not properly setting Customer expectations during the greeting and seating process, so you adjust to having the waiter give a brief explanation of how the dining experience should be.

You might also decide to add preparing glasses of ice water to the greeting and seating system instead of waiting until later in the experience. In short, look for things that are missing that would contribute to your achieving desired outcomes and figure out how to add those things.

BUILDING A NEW SYSTEM

You can use the same approach of ensuring alignment to help you build a new system. Start by defining the outcomes of the new system so it aligns with what your business needs and make sure it sits with the rest of your business.

Once the outcomes are defined, you can work backward to identify the outputs you need to achieve those outcomes, as well as the inputs and process steps needed to create those outputs.

VIEWING ALIGNMENT WITH DIFFERENT LENSES

Viewing your business through different lenses will offer alternative and helpful perspectives on your systems. Rather than as a business owner, for example, you could view your business in terms of the Customer Journey. Ask yourself about the "journey" of your Customer. Where does it start? Where does it end? What does the Customer experience along the way?

You could also view your business in terms of an employee journey. How do we find employees for our business? What is their experience like when we interview them? How do we bring new employees into our company and educate them on how we operate? How do we treat them when they are here? What are their opportunities for advancement and growth?

Alternatively, you could view your business within the context of the five pillars we talked about earlier.

There is no shortage of ways you can view the collection of systems that make up your business. But if you have done a good job of defining and aligning your outcomes, you should find consistency no matter how you decide to view your business.

However, using the different lenses to assess your business will increase your chances of finding misalignment. There should be no view of your business where systems have desired outcomes that are out of alignment with other systems for your business overall.

TO SUMMARIZE:

- Alignment of outcomes across systems reduces conflict and waste across your business.
- Alignment ensures you are doing the right things to produce the outcomes you need.
- Align your inputs to outputs and outputs to outcomes.
- Alignment will help you identify inefficiencies and gaps in your systems.
- Use this thinking to build new systems also.

Chapter 7

IDENTIFY THE SYSTEM WITH THE MOST OPPORTUNITY

IDENTIFYING the right system to work on first can be a little bit tricky. It's easy to see a problem and start work on fixing it because it's visible and in your face today – but these obvious problems are not always your most important ones.

It's also quite common to get analysis paralysis when trying to decide what to optimize first. The good news is, with a little bit of thought, you can boost your odds of picking the right thing to optimize now.

I also have a tool that you can use to help give you some guidance in picking which of your systems are more important to optimize first. This is available at resources.optimizeforoutcomes.com and we will discuss it later in the chapter. In fact, this chapter will introduce several tools to help you prioritize your optimization across systems by looking at:

- Pain that systems are causing by not achieving outcomes.
- Effort needed to address system issues.
- Impact of not removing the pain.
- Time spent vs. revenue earned.
- Upstream vs. downstream problems.

PAIN CAUSED BY NOT GETTING OUTCOMES

The first thing to consider when trying to identify the business system to improve first is to think about the pain you are feeling from each system, specific to that system not producing the desired outcomes.

Think about one of your core systems and the results it's currently giving you. Core systems are the systems that are critical to the operation of your business. How much of a gap is there between those results and your desired outcomes?

Do this for each of your core systems and note down the level of pain caused by each one.

This pain can be thought of in a few different ways. Pain might be hours wasted, upset Customers or employees from a process, or risk associated with a process going badly. These are just a few examples and are not meant to be all-inclusive. You will also need to factor in the frequency of which the pain occurs. Pain happening once a month is not as bad as pain happening every hour.

Here are a couple of examples of thinking about the pain coming from a system. First, let's imagine that you spend time every week managing and reconciling your invoices to your Clients. At the end of each month, you spend several hours reviewing the invoices and find that many have slipped through. Even worse, at the end of each year, when you go to file your taxes, you find that you missed some invoices throughout the year and that resulted in missing or lost revenue.

It would be safe to say that your invoicing system is causing you and your business great pain. You are spending many hours weekly, monthly and yearly working with invoices and still not getting good results. Much of this time is spent redoing work that you've already done, resulting in a total loss of true productivity. Clearly, that needs fixing.

For a second example, imagine you put out three social media posts per day in your business. You have a system to generate ideas, research those ideas, write the post, find a related image, and get it published. While most days you get your three posts out, things don't go well twice a month and you only produce two posts.

That you miss one post every couple of weeks is a problem, but it's not a very painful problem. It would generally rate very low in the grand scheme of all the systems working in your business.

It's obvious that the most painful systems are good candidates for any improvement efforts, but this is not the only factor in identifying where to begin.

EFFORT TO FIX OR RESOLVE ISSUES

Another major consideration is the effort involved to improve the system. While you might not know exactly what you would do at this point to make improvements, you have a general idea of how complex the system is today. The more complex the system, generally, the more effort that will be required to make improvements.

This isn't always 100 percent true but is a good guideline if you are unsure about how to rate the effort.

For example, say you want to improve the way you track leads and sales in your business. Today, you are doing this in an email, a spreadsheet, notes on your phone, and in your head. You also know that to do it your desired way, you will need to implement a CRM application and integrate it with your website and accounting software.

While you don't know every single task that you are going to need to do to complete this switch, you know that adding new software and integrating it with websites and other software is fairly complex. You can assume that the level of effort to optimize your leads and sales tracking will be high to very high.

On the opposite end of the scale, if you are thinking of making minor adjustments to a manual process you have a virtual assistant do, this would be straightforward. There is little complexity in telling the VA to do something slightly differently.

By estimating the level of complexity and effort required to make improvements, you've now added a new dimension to understanding where you should focus your optimization efforts.

If a potential improvement will solve a highly painful problem but requires a very high level of effort to do so, you might wait to make those improvements and instead pick a problem that has a medium amount of pain but can be fixed more easily.

IMPACT IF YOU DON'T REMOVE THE PAIN

Before selecting any problem as your number one thing to address, ask yourself the question: "What if I don't fix it?"

The answer to that question will further refine your list of priorities as you define problems that aren't necessarily worth fixing. You will also move more critical issues to the top of your prioritization list by identifying issues that are causing significant impacts on your business.

As an example, consider an onboarding process that is managed by a virtual assistant. Let's say this process has some problems which cause one out of every ten new Customers to leave. This would be quite impactful to your business long term and would be something to consider addressing immediately.

On the other hand, if these problems with your onboarding process required an hour of rework from your virtual assistant (VA) each month, the impact of not removing the pain is just that you will continue to pay your VA for an extra hour's worth of work each month. While wasting money intentionally is never a good idea, the impact is minor in the grand scheme of your business.

OPERATIONAL TIME INVESTED AND PROPORTION OF REVENUE

Two further considerations are the operational time that you invest in performing activities within the system and the relationship the system has in generating revenue for your business.

Consider first the operational time you invest in performing the activities within the system. If you have a system to publish one article per month on your blog or in a publication, you are probably doing many other things also and the ratio of time spent publishing an article is low compared to the time you spend on your business. On the flip side, you might be responding to 20 Customer inquiries every day, which takes up a larger percentage of the time you spend working on your business.

This begins to impact on how you should prioritize the systems that you're optimizing when you add the relationship to revenue.

In previous examples, publishing an article in a month on your blog might generate marginal traffic that leads to a couple of sales. The revenue relationship is low but so is the time that you put into that system. Answering 20 Customer inquiries daily might generate multiple sales as we answer their questions and help them with their decision-making process. While it's a large time investment, the relationship it has to your revenue is also high, so it's not necessarily a big problem.

The best situation is to have systems that take little time but drive large amounts of revenue. Systems that are already in that state need less of your attention and should be lower on the list of systems to optimize. The worst situation is systems that require large amounts of time but have little to no impact on revenue. These are prime candidates for optimizing your business and getting better outcomes.

OTHER POINTS TO CONSIDER

There is a concept in systems thinking that each of your systems is a flowing stream. Tasks that happen at the beginning of your system are referred to as happening upstream. Those happening at the end of the system are referred to as happening downstream.

Any two tasks within the system can be related as being upstream or downstream from each other.

When considering where to focus optimization efforts, fixing upstream problems and optimizing upstream process steps will often provide better results. This is because problems that occur early in a system or process often cause more problems downstream. By optimizing what is happening upstream, you better position the work happening downstream to have fewer issues. And addressing downstream issues sometimes won't make any difference in your outcomes because the real problems are happening earlier in the process.

You should also consider leveraging any metrics you have about your business wherever possible. Metrics will give you a better view of what's happening and why it's happening – so long as the effort needed to use those metrics is reasonable. Be sure to not get caught up spending weeks or months gathering metrics to try to identify where to begin your work. Oftentimes, this amount of rigor does not provide enough added value over anecdotal evidence.

On that note, be sure to avoid analysis paralysis. Set a fixed period of time (timebox) to carry out any analysis activities you have identified for prioritizing which systems to work on first. It's all too common for companies to spend weeks or months on trying to decide what their biggest problem is. In this time, they could have optimized multiple systems and made improvements that give value to their business sooner. It's better to take action on the second or third most important item than to take no action at all because you're still trying to figure out which system is number one.

The last point to make here is that these values, specific to your systems, can and will change over time. Just because something is difficult to solve today, it doesn't mean it will be difficult to solve tomorrow. As technology changes and your business changes, so too will how you answer these questions.

This goes the other way as well; just because something is easy to solve today, it doesn't mean it will be easy to solve tomorrow.

Related to this, just because something worked well in the past, it doesn't mean it's what your business needs now to get your desired outcomes. You should always be willing to consider that what worked for you in the past isn't necessarily what is going to be best for you today and be willing to make changes to get better outcomes.

THE IMPACT PRIORITIZATION TOOL

I've put together a tool to help you better prioritize your systems quickly. This is an Excel-based table that has a few formulas that will give you a priority value between one and 100 with 100 being the biggest.

Rate each of your systems on the criteria outlined in this chapter and the priority score is automatically calculated for you. This is meant to be an aid to get you optimizing your systems quickly instead of spending weeks or months gathering and analyzing data.

You can find this and other tools to help you optimize your business for better outcomes at resources.optimizeforoutcomes.com

TO SUMMARIZE:

- Identify values for the following topics for your core systems:
    - o Pain caused by poor outcomes.
    - o Effort needed to fix or resolve issues.
    - o Impact on your business if you don't optimize each system.

- The operational time spent and contribution to revenue of each system.
- Addressing upstream problems often fixes downstream issues.
- Leverage metrics where possible.
- Avoid analysis paralysis.
- Use our impact prioritization tool to help if you're stuck.

ACTIVITY

Download the Optimize For Outcomes Workbook from resources.optimizeforoutcomes.com and locate the sheet named "Impact Prioritization Tool." Put in your core systems to prioritize where you should be spending your time optimizing.

Chapter 8

OPTIMIZING YOUR SYSTEMS

WHEN businesses first start talking about optimizing their systems and processes, it's common for people to want to start by adding software to remove manual steps and automate their processes.

But automating is the last thing you should do when you are looking to optimize your business.

Automating a bad, wasteful system or process will cost more money, take you more time, and will be more expensive to maintain and manage over time. Plus, if your bigger needs or problems are related to improving effectiveness, adding automation won't do anything to help.

In this chapter, we'll explore the right way to approach optimizing your existing systems, including:

- Understanding effectiveness, efficiency, and productivity problems.
- Eliminating, then consolidating and lastly automating to gain efficiency and productivity.

REMINDER: Inputs go through process steps to create outputs. Outputs combined with other outputs and people's emotions create outcomes. All of it can be measured by defining metrics. Re-read Chapters Four and Five for an in-depth review if needed.

EFFECTIVENESS, EFFICIENCY, OR A PRODUCTIVITY PROBLEM?

The first thing to do in optimizing a system is to identify if you have an effectiveness problem or an efficiency/productivity problem. It's also possible you have a combination of two (or more) in which case you'll need to tackle the effectiveness issues first and then address efficiency and productivity.

Remember the definitions we laid out in Chapter One? Effectiveness is a measure of how well the system is meeting the defined desired outcomes. Productivity is a measure of the outputs of the system.

What you're trying to avoid here is putting energy and resources into a system and end up making things worse. Adding more inputs to a bad system isn't going to give you better results. Efficiently producing the wrong thing isn't going to make your Customers happier.

Ask if your system is giving you the outcomes you expect. If it's not, ask yourself why and think about it with a "systems thinking" mindset – that is to say, remember that the outcomes are made by a combination of system outputs and people's reactions to the outputs.

Which of the outputs are potentially causing problems in getting the outcomes? If it's the human element, why are they reacting the way they are? At this point, you might need to do a little bit of research to figure out what is really going on and why your outcomes aren't being achieved. Ultimately, you will need to identify one or more outputs that need to be different in order to achieve different outcomes (remember the relationship between inputs, process steps, outputs, and outcomes).

Here's an example: I once worked with a health coach who came to me looking to make more money. He defined his ultimate outcomes as wanting personal fulfillment with enough money to quit the corporate job he was still working to make ends meet. He was getting good results helping the people that did sign up for his services, but he was struggling to get enough business to allow him to quit his corporate job and focus on the business full time. So, we started to dissect his business in terms of systems, inputs, process steps, and outputs.

As we looked at his business in these pieces, we were able to confirm the obvious reason he was not getting enough business. It was because he didn't have enough traffic coming into his systems to generate enough sales to reach his desired outcomes. But what also became clear was that he didn't have the capacity to deliver more services (his only product at the time was him/selling consulting hours).

He didn't have the right outputs coming out of his lead generation system but also had *nothing* coming out of his product development in terms of scalable products. A scalable product would be something that he could sell that wouldn't require his time like his one-on-one coaching did. The only way he was going to generate the revenue needed to achieve the outcomes he desired was to build a product that could be sold that required less of his time to deliver.

Once your effectiveness is on point, it's time to move onto efficiency and productivity.

We look at productivity and efficiency together because they are closely related. Oftentimes, the best way to increase productivity is to increase efficiency and then turn up the volumes of your inputs.

A business's limitations can include its ability to "just do more", especially when it has manual systems and processes. Increasing productivity can often be very expensive. But by improving efficiency first, you're able to do more with less; limiting cost increases while scaling your outputs to greater levels.

FIRST, ELIMINATE

So, looking at optimizing your system or process for efficiency/productivity, the next step is to identify outputs that are not contributing to desired outcomes. If, for example, you are generating a set of reports on user metrics that don't help you better understand your systems or reach any of your defined outcomes, this is a candidate for elimination. The time you spend building, maintaining, and consuming the reports would be considered a waste.

Once you have identified those outputs, you must then consider eliminating the process steps that do not contribute to outputs. Look at each of the process steps in your system and ask: "What output is this step contributing to?" If the answer is none, then this process step is a candidate for elimination. For example, you may have your Customers fill out a web form when they buy a product from you, but the data generated is not used in any other part of your business. The time, energy, and cost associated with maintaining the form and the data is going to waste and should be eliminated.

Moving on, your next task is to look at inputs that can be eliminated. Analyze each of the inputs with an eye for identifying those that do not contribute to outputs or outcomes. For example, if you have a system for creating ads and as part of that you gather stock photos as well as memes, but you find yourself always selecting a meme, you should quit spending the time to gather the stock photos and remove them as an input into your process.

The last thing to consider while you are eliminating things is any step in your system that isn't adding value that a Customer would pay for. In the world of process improvement, this would be referred to as a non-value-added step. When you do this, take a ruthless definition of the term non-value-added. If a Customer will not pay you more for your product as a result of the step, it is non-value-added.

Understand that this strict definition will mean most of what you do as a business is non-value-added to the Customer. The reality is most businesses and most systems include many process steps that aren't valuable to the Customer, but some of these non-value-added steps are critical to your business (such as paying taxes), so you aren't going to eliminate them. But taking this strict view of non-value-added steps will help you see what you need to do and what you might be able to eliminate.

NEXT, CONSOLIDATE

Once you have eliminated any inputs, process steps, or outputs to ensure you are doing the things that matter the most, the next step is to consolidate where you can. Consolidating in this sense means looking at the outputs and outcomes you are trying to achieve and reducing the number of ways you are working to produce them.

Here's an example. I worked with a Client who was managing leads in three different ways. Each way can be labeled a different "workstream." This business used email to manage and track interactions with potential Customers. Folders were set up for each lead and any communication with the Customer was put into his or her respective folder. The company also used a spreadsheet to manage and track leads that came in from trade shows. This spreadsheet contained some details about who the lead was, who the lead worked for, what product they were interested in, etc. Sometimes these leads ended up getting tracked through email as well, but oftentimes never left the spreadsheet as the interactions were done primarily via phone for leads that came from trade shows. This company also had a web form associated with a lead magnet that generated leads. These leads were managed through the website and a different email address by a different assistant than used to manage the other email-based leads.

You can see that's not the best way of doing things, right?

In this case, a lightweight CRM application allowed the business to consolidate all their leads in one location. They were still able to track all the details they wanted to for different leads and lead sources but it also gave them a single, standard workstream for how they managed all of their leads instead of managing three different workstreams.

Another method for consolidating is to reduce the number of tactics used to achieve a shared desired outcome. It's not uncommon to see a business doing many different things to try to achieve a single desired outcome. While this isn't always bad, it can lead to wasted effort and less than desirable results.

Let's imagine a business that operates on 12 social media platforms to find leads. But this is a small business and they can only do a mediocre job across all 12 platforms because they don't have the resources to do them all well. They have diluted their focus by trying to be everywhere in the assumption that a larger presence will give them more leads and better outcomes. The truth is, with fewer resources, they would be better off choosing a couple of social platforms and doing them well. That would achieve better outcomes with a narrower focus.

A third tactic used to consolidate is to look at different inputs to see if you can combine them. Returning to a previous example, imagine an advertising system that uses memes as well as static images with no text. This requires management of separate yet very similar images, some which have text and some which do not. Could the business use only memes for their advertising and still get the same results? This would simplify their image catalog, requiring fewer images to be maintained.

Here's another example. Imagine a restaurant that uses three different colored tablecloths with separate napkins and placemats to match each color. While there is probably a good reason that they decided to do this, could they consolidate and use the same colors for all their table-cloths? While this might sound minor and perhaps insignificant, if it takes an extra five minutes to coordinate and manage different colors per table, and the restaurant is setting 100 tables per day, that's more than eight hours per day wasted matching colors. It also takes time and en-ergy to manage the different colors (sorting, ordering new, storing, washing, etc.) that would be saved by consolidating colors.

LAST, AUTOMATE

Once you've eliminated waste and consolidated similar workstreams and inputs, you are ready to start automating to gain additional benefits by optimizing your systems.

By eliminating and consolidating first, you have reduced the amount of time and energy required to automate and you will end up with an easier to manage system when all is said and done. If you hadn't eliminated and consolidated first, you'd be spending extra time and money automating redundant tasks.

Before you start automation work, it's important to understand the options that you have to automate your systems.

Standalone applications exist that will help you automate large processes. For example, there are many options for building automated email sequences to help you engage with your audience. These applications can be configured so emails and attachments will automatically send at certain time intervals based on certain event triggers.

For many parts of your business, applications will likely exist to help you partially or fully automate the systems and processes that you run. From scheduling Clients to invoicing and accounting, and everything in between, there are applications to help you automate.

A second approach to automation involves directly connecting two or more applications. Many applications come with out-of-the-box connectors that can be configured with a few clicks. For example, Gravity Forms is an application that runs on a WordPress website. Gravity Forms has a connector that allows you to link a form on your website directly to different CRM applications. This means that when a user completes the form on your site, their information is automatically entered into your CRM application, saving you from having to enter the information manually.

Some tools act as bridges that can also help you connect two or more applications. Zapier, for example, is a connector application that allows you to build connections between hundreds of different software applications just by clicking some options. It's quick and easy to use and requires no code to be written to complete an integration between different applications.

Using Zapier, you could connect a Gmail account to a Google Sheet so that any time email is received, Zapier will automatically fill in the spreadsheet with certain details from the email.

This is just one simple example of what these types of applications can do but there are hundreds, if not thousands, of use cases for how you can automate two different applications together.

A third option is to build a custom integration by writing code. This is not a cheap or easy option and is not something you want to do without good guidance. It should also only be considered after you've exhausted all paths with options one and two. It requires a software developer and can be time-consuming due to the complexities of integrating applications with code.

Building custom integrations between applications is not the only way a software developer can help with automation. Software developers can also write custom code to automate any part of your business where a third-party application doesn't already exist.

Some applications, especially the larger ones, have environments that allow a developer to write custom code on top of the application. For example, the CRM application salesforce.com has a development environment that allows a developer to build additional applications on top of its data and processes.

Developers can also build standalone applications to automate any part of your business. Again, this is an expensive and more complicated option than some of the other options already discussed and you shouldn't go down this path without some guidance from someone who understands software development. Also, expect that a custom application will cost you many thousands of dollars for a simple application.

COMING BACK TO PRODUCTIVITY

Now your system is optimized, you can turn up the volume of inputs to increase your outputs/productivity.

By optimizing for efficiency first, you have removed the waste in your systems and processes so that as you scale your business, you're not scaling this waste along with it.

Here's an example of this in action. I started working with a guy called Duke in February of 2019. He wanted to grow his coaching business but his great start had plateaued into flat/no growth.

We focused first on identifying the activities he was performing in his business that weren't contributing to the outcomes he wanted. We eliminated waste, removed programs that were consuming loads of time with little return, consolidated work where possible, and then automated what was left.

Once we had optimized his systems to improve efficiency, he was able to crank up the volume of the productivity of his team, increasing his revenue three-fold, while reducing his overhead costs. Hear more from Duke in his own words at www.optimizeforoutcomes.com/testimonials.

TO SUMMARIZE:

- Identify if you have an effectiveness, productivity, or efficiency problem in your system.
- Tackle effectiveness first since efficiently producing ineffective products doesn't help you.
- Work through efficiency and productivity problems together as they are closely related.
- First eliminate, then consolidate, and lastly automate.
- Eliminate inputs, processes, and outputs that are not contributing to your desired outcomes.
- Consolidate workstreams, processes, and inputs to fewer variations.
- Automate last to save yourself from automating unneeded process steps.
- Once your systems and processes are more efficient, scaling becomes easier and you don't scale waste with your business.

Chapter 9

MANAGING CHANGE

THERE is an entire discipline around managing change properly so that the change sticks and becomes the new norm. It is worth understanding some basics to make sure any optimizations you do for your business stay around and provide value well into the future. Change management is an expansive topic, so we will cover only the basics here.

Change can be hard for anybody. As humans, we like comfortable and we like stable. Things that are comfortable and stable bring us a sense of security, while change is a contradictory force to that comfort and stability. In any aspect of life, change can be hard to introduce and to maintain to the point of new habits forming – and change in business is no different.

In this chapter, we'll discuss:

- When to start managing change.
- Tactics for actively managing change.
- How to use metrics to track adoption of changes.

WHEN TO START MANAGING CHANGE

Managing change should start properly well before the change takes place. If you are thinking about adding a new application to your business, your change management should start at the time you decide to add the software and not at the time it is implemented.

This is true for any change you want to make – the process begins when you decide to change, not when you implement the change.

You need to think about all the different stakeholders that could be affected by any change you make in your business. Even if you are a solo entrepreneur, it may impact your Customers, a vendor that you use to provide a service, or even your family members if it means big changes for you personally.

It is important to clarify who these affected stakeholders are and start managing their expectations about upcoming change well before it happens.

One thing to do is to involve the people that will be impacted in the decision-making around the change. For example, if you are working to change the way you deliver products to your Customers, ask them to get involved before you make any final decisions. You could do this by surveying your Customers about new features or changes you are thinking of making to your website. You could build a prototype of the new experience and ask a few to test it out for you. There are many ways to start involving those who will be impacted before anything is changed.

Whether it's Customers, employees, vendors, or people around you in your personal life, the more you can bring them in before any changes occur, the better you will be able to set their expectations of upcoming changes. The more a person feels like they were part of the change and that it was at least partly their idea, the more likely they are to stick with it and see it through. They are less likely to complain if the change is "their idea" as opposed to someone else forcing them to change.

Note that you must be a little bit careful about how you do this because it can do more harm than good if approached the wrong way.

If you are already set in your mind as to exactly what is changing and you ask affected stakeholders for their feedback but don't like any of their suggestions, you will potentially create hard feelings by implementing a change that people didn't want/like. You will need to either modify your change based on the feedback or come prepared to make solid arguments as to why your changes are needed.

Another tactic for managing change before the change happens is to lay out a communication plan. This should address how you plan to communicate with anybody and everybody affected by the change you plan on making. This might include how processes will change, new expectations people should have, or things that individuals need to do differently, among other things. Communications should be scheduled and ongoing throughout the change process.

Let's go back to our example of changing the way products are delivered to a Customer. The change management plan might include early communications that happen months ahead of the change, making our Customers aware that a change is coming, and soliciting feedback. You could follow that up after a week or two with additional communication highlighting some of the most important feedback and how you are adapting the change based on what input the Customers provided.

Additional follow-up communications could happen between the initial few alerts and the actual change happening that highlight the progress you are making towards effecting the change. Once the change goes live, you'll want to continue your communication until the change becomes the new habit.

AFTER THE CHANGE

After you make changes, it is important to keep your finger on the pulse to ensure that you and others don't fall back into old habits. You should continue to have and execute on a communications plan, keeping those involved informed and reminding them what they should be doing now.

You can also use this as an opportunity to gain additional feedback on how you executed the change and how the change is impacting people. If you've implemented a change as an individual, be sure to do some self-reflection as you won't have feedback from other stakeholders.

It is important to note that the level of rigor used to manage change is highly dependent on many factors. If a change is small and doesn't impact many people, then obviously you do not want to spend 100 hours building and managing a communication plan. If a change is massive, complicated, and impacts 1,000 people, you should be spending more than 15 minutes to plan it out. Use good judgment here and reach out to others if you're unsure.

METRICS AND MONITORING

Having basic metrics on your business is critical to any optimization or improvement program. You must be able to see the results of what you're doing to understand if you are doing the right things or the wrong things. Without any metrics, it's all just a guessing game and none of it matters.

Metrics do not have to be complicated or fancy. They can be as simple as jotting down a couple of data points every day or week about a particular system or process. You don't need millions of metrics or fancy business intelligence dashboards to get value out of tracking metrics.

There are two great examples where the importance of metrics is easily shown. First, imagine walking into a gym because you want to improve your health and fitness. You meet a trainer and they start to ask you some basic questions, such as how much you sleep at night, your average daily caloric intake, and how much and what types of exercises you are already doing. These are a few of the things that you would be asked to get a baseline understanding of where you are and what you're doing.

You'd work with the trainer to identify your goals and come up with a plan on how to get there that would focus on you doing specific exercises for certain durations and eating specific foods. This information would be tracked in some sort of log to keep a record of your progress.

By looking at the metrics, the trainer can make adjustments as you go to make sure you meet your goals in the timeframe that you want to meet them. If you are not gaining enough muscle fast enough, the trainer will increase the calories you're eating. If your strength is not increasing at the right pace, the trainer will adjust your exercises. Only by understanding some basic metrics is the trainer able to see what's happening and make the right adjustments.

Now imagine telling the trainer you "don't do metrics". How is anyone going to know if you are gaining or losing weight? How are they going to know if you are on the right path to meet the goals you have in the timeframe you defined? How is the trainer going to know what tweaks to make to get you to the right spot? The answer is that the trainer won't have any idea. They will be guessing and hoping for the best. This is not a great way to get healthier – and it's not a great way to run your business, either.

It's also important to measure the right thing because "vanity metrics" can lead you to the wrong understanding of a system's performance. In the world of fitness, weight can often be thought of as a vanity metric. If you wanted to get healthier and decided that meant losing weight, you could end up starving yourself and lose a bunch of weight, but actually be in worse health than before you started. In reality, becoming healthier could mean you gain weight even though you lose inches from your waist and improve your overall appearance.

In business, you can get caught up in vanity metrics that don't really give you a good measure of the quality of your system. You could run ads that get thousands of likes and engagement, but lots of likes doesn't necessarily indicate a healthy business or system.

Another example has to do with personal finances. If you've ever taken a class, read a book, or been instructed by anyone to improve your financial situation, what is the first thing you are told to do? Put together some baseline numbers, most likely. How much are you spending on your rent or mortgage? How much do you spend per month on utilities?

Some basic metrics are established based on your money coming in and money going out. Without this information, a financial planner is unable to provide any real advice or assistance in getting you to a better place. Nobody would think that they could change their financial picture without paying attention to some baseline metrics and making decisions on what to improve based on those metrics. Your business is no different.

WHEN AND WHAT TO MEASURE

You should always be measuring, but the question of what to measure is a little bit more challenging. You don't need to measure everything all the time to be successful, and you certainly don't want to drown yourself in metrics so that it draws too much attention away from the other activities you need to have a successful business.

You probably already have some metrics today even if you don't realize it. Most modern software has data and reporting that allows you to look at different elements of why it is you are using the software. For example, any CRM is going to have data around the contacts you have in the system. You can likely get reports out of your CRM today that show you sales conversion rates, new leads added per month, and many other sales-related metrics.

But to decide exactly what to measure, you need to do a little bit of thinking about your desired outcomes of your business and each of your systems. You need to think about how your systems operate and what you could reasonably measure from those systems. Then, define the metrics you need for each system to understand that the system is performing the way it should and giving you the outcomes that you have defined.

Here's an example. Consider a system designed to convert leads into sales. The desired outcome of the system is to close sales with Customers that are ecstatic to use the product they just purchased. Think about how you could measure Customers being ecstatic to use the product.

It depends, somewhat, on what the product is, so let's say it's a digital product which could be a book download, a course, special group access, etc. A Customer who is ecstatic to use their new product would likely use a digital product very soon after purchase, if not immediately. A metric that would tell us the time between purchase and the Customer downloading or accessing their digital product would be a good indicator of how ecstatic they were to use the product. If the Customer waited two weeks to open their new audiobook, arguably they weren't ecstatic to get it. Another option might be to create a simple survey that gets sent to Customers three days after they purchase. The results from the survey could be tracked over time and reviewed as metrics of how ecstatic Customers were when they bought the product.

The point here is that there are usually multiple options rather than one right answer. The other takeaway is that it doesn't have to be complicated or crazy. One or two metrics are good enough to get started. You'll be much better off with something than nothing, but you don't want to waste all your time building metrics to get that something.

POINT-IN-TIME VERSUS ONGOING METRICS

Some metrics only need to be a snapshot in time to be effective. This is to say that you don't have to track the metrics day in, day out over many months to get value out of them. Sometimes, measuring for a day or a week will give you enough information about where you have hurdles to overcome that you don't need to continue to measure.

I regularly ask Clients to spend a week tracking how they spend their time. They break it down into 15 or 30-minute increments and track a day at a time. At the end of the week, we analyze where their time went and what value that time contributed to the desired outcomes of various systems and their business overall.

This is usually enough information to make solid recommendations on improvements needed to optimize how they are spending their time.

So, nobody tracks their time during the second week while they are figuring out which improvements to make and implementing them.

In fact, time won't be tracked again until meaningful changes are made and an expectation is established that the time profile will look different. Sometimes, this might be two months after the initial tracking week.

But once changes are made, it is appropriate to do the time study again and track how time is being spent in the business. From the second round, analysis can be carried out to determine whether or not the changes made had any impact on improving the way time is spent in the business. If there are still major problems, another round of analysis and changes would be appropriate. Oftentimes, the changes made from the first round are "enough for now" and we move on to other priorities.

It's good to go back periodically and check any of these one-time metrics. It could be as infrequent as once every six months, but checking regularly will make sure you stay on track.

When you make a change in your business, processes tend to "drift" over time. People initially get excited about the change management and are heavily focused on doing it differently, but they tend to gradually fall back to their old habits and old ways of doing things. However, checking in with your one-time metrics every now and then will ensure that this drift happens less and that you correct it when it does happen.

ONGOING METRICS

Ongoing metrics are usually (and preferably) generated by systems as part of doing business. Manually tracking ongoing metrics can be somewhat painful, error-prone, and it's easy to forget to do them – reducing the integrity of your data.

As an example, think of an application used to facilitate end-user or Customer support. These applications usually include some sort of system where tickets are created that represent issues or problems users are having. Any modern application will have metrics built-in that cover the number of tickets created, the time tickets were created, how long it took between a ticket being opened and a ticket being closed, etc.

There is often enough data inherently in these systems that you don't need to do any additional metric capturing to give you a good indication of the health of the related system. In the case of our Customer support system, you should be able to see that, on average, you are taking two weeks to resolve a Customer's problem. How does that align with the desired outcomes you have set for your Customer support system? If it's within range, that's a good indicator that you're doing things well. If it's outside of your range, it's an indicator that you need to do some things to improve that system.

TO SUMMARIZE:

- Change management is an important part of optimizing for the long term.
- Without change management, changes that you make are likely to be undone over time.
- Identify and involve people that will be impacted by the changes you are making.
- Communicate with those who will be impacted throughout the change process from the initial idea to well after the change has been implemented.
- Use metrics to understand the impact a change has had on your process, system, or business.
- Metrics should give you an indicator of the health of your processes and systems.
- Metrics that are automatically captured as part of your work are preferred but not always available.

Chapter 10

CONTINUOUSLY IMPROVE WHERE IT MATTERS

WORKING on your business doesn't end after taking a single improvement effort. Continually improving and adapting to changes in markets, Customer behaviors, technology, and more are the only ways your business will stay successful in the future.

In this final chapter, we'll discuss the idea of continuous improvement and what to do after you've applied the learnings of Chapters One through Nine to your business.

CONTINUOUS IMPROVEMENT IS CONTINUOUS

Like many things in business, optimizing for outcomes is best served with consistency. You will get better results doing a little bit each day than you will with one big exercise once a quarter.

Think about it like brushing your teeth. If you brushed your teeth once a month for eight hours straight and went to the dentist four times a year, your teeth would fall out pretty quickly. But by brushing your teeth a couple of minutes each day, twice a day and going to the dentist twice a year, you're going to spend less time taking care of your teeth and get much better results.

Similarly, when you have finished reading each of these chapters and applying what you have learned to your business, you will be in a better place than when you started.

From here, go back to Chapter Seven and go through the process from there again. You can reuse the legwork you did from the beginning of the book and don't need to repeat Chapters One through Six for now.

As a reminder, Chapter Seven was about identifying the system that has the most opportunity for improvement. Look again at the list you created as part of that chapter and now adjust it for the improvements that you've made since you first made the list. What stands out now as the system needing the most improvement? It could still be that same system or another may have risen to the top as the area with the most opportunity to optimize. Whichever it is, continue through the steps again and make improvements to that system. You can repeat the process between Chapters Seven and Nine to identify which systems have the biggest opportunity to improve.

Occasionally, you will want to go back and review Chapters One through Six. This will allow you to add any new systems that you create along the way, as well as to re-evaluate old systems and ensure your prioritization stays correct. It also allows you to adjust the desired outcomes of the different systems and realign things as your business changes and your needs change over the coming months and years.

FINAL THOUGHTS

Once you've learned the basics of the tools and techniques for improvement, you will be able to use them in any situation. That's the beauty of these tools. Whether you are a one-person start-up, a small company, or a large corporation, the methods you have learned are useful to you and your business.

You don't have to be in a certain industry, and you don't have to be a certain type of company.

Remember that all companies are 80 to 90 percent the same. This also means that the techniques you pick up from this book will work with you as your business grows and still be just as applicable in the future.

Another pointer for effectively using the information in this book is that you don't always need to look at every system in your company to move on to making improvements. It's quite possible that you have one system that you know is broken and not giving you good outcomes. There would be little point in going through the process of mapping out your entire business and prioritizing all your systems to identify the one you already know is broken. Simply take the information in Chapters Eight and Nine and apply it to the broken system to see improvements sooner rather than later.

Like with most things, the more you practice this process for optimizing, the better you'll get at it. Don't worry about getting it perfect the first time as you will undoubtedly find your own tricks to making your business better.

Use this book as a guide and make adjustments for your situation. By doing so, you will be able to make the improvements you need for the long-term success of your business by Optimizing for Outcomes.

Find more resources online to help you optimize your business for better outcomes by visiting us at www.optimizeforoutcomes.com.

ROOT CAUSE ANALYSIS AND THE FIVE WHYS

LEARNING how to do root cause analysis through a technique known as "the five whys" has been so crucial in my professional career.

In short, root cause analysis means looking at a problem initially as a symptom and trying to dig deeper to understand the problem's root cause.

Your initial problem is most likely a symptom of something else. So, if you go in and solve the initial problem, you are likely only covering over a symptom of something much worse. You get nowhere near the real issue causing you challenges. As you work to optimize your business, understanding root cause analysis and how to apply the technique of the five whys will greatly enhance your ability to solve problems once and for all, instead of patching symptoms that continually reappear as different problems.

The five whys technique is a reminder to continue to ask yourself why something is happening until you get to the point you feel comfortable that you have identified the root cause.

As an example, think about a Customer buying a new car. Let's say that shortly after buying that new car, the paint starts to chip and the Customer returns to the dealer unhappy and wanting a solution to his problem. The paint chipping on his car isn't the problem but is a symptom of a larger problem you cannot identify without deeper thinking.

The dealer could "solve" this problem by repainting the car but, by doing so, is only putting a Band-Aid on a bigger problem. If the solution is to repaint every time the paint is chipped, the dealer will be repainting cars into the foreseeable future, which will see him or her continuing to waste time and money patching symptoms and not solving problems.

By asking yourself why, you start to dive deeper and understand the root of what is causing the paint problem to occur. Why is the paint chipping off the car? Because the new paint we're using doesn't bond to the metal like the old paint. Why does the new paint not bond like the old paint? Because the new paint is a cheaper brand and lower quality.

Just by asking why two more times, we get a much better answer as to why Customers are complaining about paint chipping on their new cars. We can also see that reapplying the paint would continue to lead to the same problems and not solve anything. If the paint itself is causing the problem, reapplying more of it will only give a temporary fix and it will soon begin to chip again since we did nothing to address the root cause.

But with that deeper understanding, we can address the root cause by changing the paint back or maybe adding a bonding agent so that it lasts longer. This will help resolve our problem without having to repaint cars in the future. By taking a short time to identify the root cause at the outset, we can save both time and money solving problems upstream and optimize the process to produce better outcomes.

The "five" in the five whys is a recommendation and not a hard and fast rule. Sometimes, you only need to ask why once. Other times, you might have to ask seven times before you get to the right place to solve the right problem. This is somewhat of a judgment call but one technique is to keep asking why until your answer either doesn't make rational sense to try to fix or you know you are unable to address that as a root cause.

With our car and paint example, we might ask why we are using a cheaper, lower quality paint. The answer may be that it's because our cars are too expensive to build. While this is insightful for management and useful in understanding overall what we need to do to solve our business problems, it doesn't necessarily help us solve our paint issue. We would consider this answer as we tried to solve our paint problems cost-effectively so that we could build cars at a lower cost but not have paint chipping for our Customers.

We could go deeper by asking why our cars are so expensive to build. In a real situation, this answer could go many ways. But, for the sake of our example, let's say the answer is because steel prices from our supplier have increased significantly over the last 12 months. We now have another piece of information that is useful overall for managing our business and it could impact the way we address our paint problem. Perhaps, instead of trying to save money on paint, we should consider using an alternate supplier to provide us with similar quality steel at a lower cost.

As you can see, continuing to ask why can provide additional insights that help us solve problems and help us get better overall as a business.

We could continue to ask why and eventually get into things like iron production being problematic in certain regions due to new mining legislation. However, as a car dealership, we won't have any ability to address that problem, so then we work our way back through the whys to a problem that we can resolve or influence.

USING SWIMLANE DIAGRAMS TO DOCUMENT A PROCESS OR SYSTEM

A SWIMLANE diagram is a common tool in the world of process management and improvement. It is a diagram that depicts a business process with each step falling in a lane of the person, team, or system responsible for performing the step. It results in a diagram that looks like a swimming pool. See the below picture for an example.

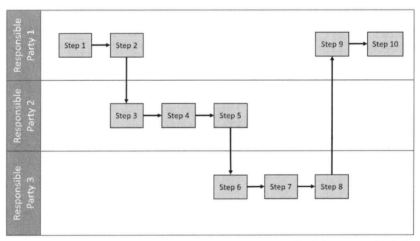

The "swim lanes" run left to right in the diagram. Each lane on the left-hand side has the person, team, or system that is responsible for each lane. Note that if you use a person, you should use their role and not their name so that your document stays correct in case the person changes roles or leaves your organization. Each box represents a step in the process with lines drawn between boxes to show how the process flows from start to finish.

A good swimlane diagram uses different shaped boxes to distinguish between certain elements of the process. There are standard uses for certain shapes that should always be used in every situation. For example, the oval is used to designate the beginning or end of a process. A rectangle is a process step. The diamond is used to designate a decision point where the process splits into two or more paths based on the decision made.

While there are other standard shapes, and it's OK to use them, be cautious that you don't use too many in your diagrams. I have seen some that use 20 different shapes to designate different things. If you get carried away like this, people will have difficulty interpreting all your shapes and what you are trying to convey. It's better to keep it simple and limit yourself to the four or five most commonly used shapes.

You can also use color to highlight different boxes. This is an alternative method to differentiate information about process steps that you wish to communicate to those reading your diagrams. For example, I use red to indicate the steps in the process that are considered value-added and gray-blue to represent non-value-added steps. Remember our definition of non-value-added from Chapter Eight? These are steps that we do even though the Customer isn't going to pay us more money for the final product because of them (e.g. paying tax). This helps us visually see where we might be able to eliminate process steps to get more efficient.

Building a swimlane diagram is an effective way to see how your process flows to identify possible bottlenecks and rework that are wasting your time and making you less efficient. It also helps you understand transitions between the parties responsible for carrying out the steps, which are commonly a source of problems in a process.

A swimlane diagram by itself does have limited usability. It is often best paired with either a process narrative or a SIPOC to provide a more comprehensive view of the process. SIPOC is a tool that comes from Six Sigma and is an acronym that stands for Supplier, Inputs, Process step, Outputs, Customer.

You shouldn't feel like you need to draw swimlane diagrams for every single one of your processes. It's a helpful tool if you are trying to make a process better and can be used to help communicate the way a process is done, but it is not the only way to do those things.

Visit us at www.optimizeforoutcomes.com/resources to download our sample tools and get further instruction on how to use these tools to help you Optimize for Outcomes.

WHAT TO DO NOW?

IF you followed along with the activities from the earlier chapters, you will be a bit ahead on what to do next. If not, that's OK too. Below, you will find step-by-step instructions on what to do next to better optimize your business for better outcomes.

No matter who you are or where you're at in your journey, you can reach me online at brian@optimizeforoutcomes.com. You can also find me on my Facebook page at https://www.facebook.com/OptimizeForOutcomes/

FOR THE BRAND-NEW ENTREPRENEUR

This is for you if you don't really have any systems today. You may be just starting out and have an idea that you think can be a business, or you've been able to generate some business but haven't taken the time to put any structure in place.

1. Define the ultimate desired outcomes of your business (use our worksheet to help you).
2. Think of your Customer's journey:
   a. How will you generate traffic?
   b. How will you convert that traffic into sales?
   c. How will you deliver and support your product?
   d. How will you track the basics in your business (sales, payments, taxes, etc.)?
   e. How will you manage and prioritize tasks?
3. The answers to those five questions are your first five systems. Define desired outcomes for each of them and make sure these align with your desired ultimate outcomes.
4. For each system:

a. Define the outputs you need to get the outcomes.
b. Define the inputs you need to get the outputs.
c. Define the sources for the inputs.
d. Define the process for transforming the inputs to the outputs.
e. Define the metrics that will be used to measure the health of the system.
5. Use a SIPOC and process narrative to help define each system.

You should be able to complete this in a couple hours at most. If it's taking you longer, you're overthinking it. These are living documents and you can add to them/improve over time.

Once you've got your systems defined and documented, you are ready to start building out your systems.

FOR THE ESTABLISHED BUSINESS

1. Define the ultimate desired outcomes of your business (use our worksheet to help you).
2. Define your core (important) systems. This will be different for each business, but you should be able to identify which systems are critical to your business's success.
3. Define desired outcomes for each of them and make sure these align with your desired ultimate outcomes.
4. Use the Impact Prioritization Tool to identify the problems you're currently having and the relative priority of each.
5. For the top priority system:
   a. Document the system as it is today including inputs, process steps, and outputs. Use a process narrative, swimlane diagram, SIPOC, or any combination of the three.
   b. Create a change management plan that will help you manage stakeholder communication.

c. Identify if you have an effectiveness, productivity, or efficiency problem (or a combination):
   i. Effectiveness – are you getting the outcomes?
   ii. Productivity – does the system supply of outputs meet demand?
   iii. Efficiency – do the outputs cost too many resources (inputs) to make?
d. Solve effectiveness problems first:
   i. Identify outputs that are not contributing in the right way to your outcomes.
   ii. Adjust the inputs and process steps that are creating the output to give you better outputs.
   iii. Add new outputs if needed.
e. Solve efficiency and productivity problems together since they are closely related:
   i. Identify and eliminate non-value-added outputs, steps, and inputs.
   ii. Consolidate like inputs and workstreams.
   iii. Automate with technology to remove manual processes.
f. Define the metrics that will be used to measure the health of the system.

6. Execute your plans and make the adjustments needed.
7. Monitor your metrics to make sure changes turn into habits and stick.
8. Go to Step 4 and repeat Steps 4 to 8. Occasionally go back to Step 1 and redo the whole process.

SPECIFIC SYSTEM PROBLEM RESOLUTION

You might have a specific system that you know isn't working well today and instead of taking the time to go through and document all your core systems, you just need to improve the one system starting today.

If that is the case, these are the steps for you:

1. Define the desired outcomes of the system and ensure it aligns to your overall business desired outcomes (use the ultimate outcome worksheet to define your overall business desired outcomes if needed).
2. Document the system as it is today including inputs, process steps, and outputs. Use a process narrative, swimlane diagram, SIPOC, or any combination of the three.
3. Create a change management plan that will help you manage stakeholder communication.
4. Identify if you have an effectiveness, productivity, or efficiency problem (or a combination):
   a. Effectiveness – are you getting the outcomes?
   b. Productivity – does the system supply of outputs meet demand?
   c. Efficiency – do the outputs cost too many resources (inputs) to make?
5. Solve effectiveness problems first:
   a. Identify outputs that are not contributing in the right way to your outcomes.
   b. Adjust the inputs and process steps that are creating the output to give you better outputs.
   c. Add new outputs if needed.
6. Solve efficiency and productivity problems together since they are closely related:
   a. Identify and eliminate non-value-added outputs, steps, and inputs.
   b. Consolidate like inputs and workstreams.
   c. Automate with technology to remove manual processes.
7. Define the metrics that will be used to measure the health of the system.
8. Execute your plans and make the adjustments needed.
9. Monitor your metrics to make sure changes turn into habits and stick.

THE SMALL COMPANY LOOK-ING TO SCALE

IN 2019, I started working with a health and lifestyle coach who had a desire to scale his business and make more money. He had seven employees and had been in business for a few years. He was doing OK financially but wanted to grow the business so he could help more people and pay his staff more. He had been trying to grow for a couple of years but couldn't get over the roadblocks to scaling.

He couldn't even identify what it was that was preventing him from growing the business bigger.

Revenue was generated through charging members monthly for access to a private Facebook group. Anyone who joined the group also got access to a video library of courses the business had created. This was the sole source of income. He also ran occasional in-person events, but these were either free or had a minimal charge to cover just the cost associated with the event and never made him any money.

IDENTIFYING SYSTEMS AND DESIRED OUTCOMES

We started going through his business systems to identify the core systems that he and his team managed to make the business function. He identified a few areas where the team spent most of their time. This included running advertising campaigns, onboarding new Clients, managing the Facebook group, and managing events.

These were also the systems that he identified as having the most opportunity for improvement. He estimated that 90 percent of his team's time was spent in these few areas. There were other systems called out, but these were of minor significance and not prioritized as systems with good opportunities for optimization.

In addition to the systems, we took an inventory of software applications. There were applications to manage the videos, marketing campaigns, and email sequences. Google Docs was highly leveraged as a way to pass information between his employees.

We went through and identified the desired outcomes for each of these systems. Advertising campaigns were being run to find people in the right state of mind at the right time in their lives to benefit from his services. Onboarding new Clients was a fairly lengthy process spanning the course of several weeks that was designed to educate people on the tools and techniques that would help them be better prepared to deal with life's challenges. Managing the Facebook group was done to provide an environment where his Clients could interact, learn from each other, and share their wins and struggles.

The desired outcome of the events he ran was to add more people to his community and educate them on his tools and techniques.

We had also defined the ultimate outcomes he was looking for in managing his business. He wanted money, but mostly as a way to enrich the lives of others and achieve the personal fulfillment that was really driving his business. He also wanted a sense of fulfillment from helping others to learn tools and techniques that would help them in their daily lives. He wanted to scale the business to generate more money to pay his existing staff more for their hard work and to be able to spread his message, tools, and techniques to larger audiences.

Our next step was to align the desired outcomes of the individual systems to his desired ultimate outcomes. What became obvious as we did this was that all the outcomes he defined for his individual systems aligned very well to his personal fulfillment goals. However, he had no defined outcomes related to increasing the business's income.

While it sounds obvious in hindsight, this was his first realization of why he was having difficulty growing the revenue of the business. Despite what he was telling himself in his mind, he wasn't taking action anywhere to actually grow revenues.

To correct this, we opened the discussion up to talk about ideas on how we would modify systems in his business with the desired outcomes of generating additional revenue.

For example, we adjusted his desired outcomes for managing his Facebook group to include "in a manner that generates positive cash flow for the business". Now the goals of managing the Facebook group were not just to create an environment where his Clients can interact, but to do so in a way that also made his business money.

We also talked about how we would implement new systems that would help contribute to his goals. For example, nobody in his business was putting any time or thought into the development of new features for his existing products or the development of new products. Everything was just the way it was and there was no effort put into adjusting for changing market conditions. He decided to add a new product development system that would be able to refine his existing products and help him identify and deliver new products to his Customers.

At this point, we hadn't even optimized anything but had already been able to identify one of the major problems preventing him from growing his business. We identified a mindset shift needed to increase his revenues based on his existing business. We also identified a new system that would provide good value in helping him achieve his desired outcomes that he wasn't currently getting.

GATHERING DATA FOR ANALYSIS

One of the first things this entrepreneur did with his team was to carry out a time study for a week. He had everyone on his team enter in 30-minute increments about what system they were working in and what they were doing. We also had the team write out the process steps for each of these systems; what they were doing and in what order were they were performing the steps.

.

On day one of the team tracking their activities, the realizations of where time was being wasted was immediate. Because of our initial conversations, people were already thinking about the need to perform activities that contributed to the desired outcomes and created the value expected. They realized they were spending time on things that returned little or no value.

This is something that I've seen time and time again. Oftentimes, just the act of doing a time study will highlight where someone is being inefficient and lead to improvements without doing anything else.

After a week, we had a good amount of data to analyze to see how the team was spending their time. We grouped the team's entries by the system associated with each entry. As we went through the data, we could start to paint a picture of where individuals were spending too much time and where they were spending not enough time.

For example, in managing the Facebook group, there were instances of individual calls with staff members that took up to three hours to complete. While these calls were good for that personal fulfillment in helping people, they were contributing nothing to the revenue of the business.

Customer onboarding was another area where it was immediately clear that the team was spending a lot of time for little to no return.

As I previously mentioned, the onboarding of new Clients took several weeks as part of an initial education program. Each week, there were homework assignments and the team members were spending hours trying to track who completed what. If a Client hadn't completed something, staff would spend more time writing them emails, sending the messages, or calling to discuss why they hadn't done the work and what could be done to help.

Oftentimes, the Client didn't need anything and just didn't have time that week to complete the assignment. In these cases, the team wasted their time following up on something that didn't need attention.

MAKING CHANGES

With this information, the business made some changes to some of their policies and how they operated their business. We first looked at the system for managing the Facebook group.

Overall, the system was only partially effective in achieving our newly defined desired outcomes. The system was giving Customers the interactions and community desired, but it was not doing so in a way that generated a positive ROI for the business.

First, resources were created to help Customers self-serve on a number of issues that previously would have resulted in messages or long phone calls that consumed staff time. This was done in a way to not take any perceived value away from the Customer's viewpoint.

Internally, processes were adjusted so that getting on the phone with a Customer was the last resort. Other resources were leveraged first that allowed the staff to resolve most issues in a matter of seconds. When calls did happen, protocols were put in place to minimize the amount of time spent talking with Customers on the phone by focusing on the right topics to get the Customers the value they were looking for.

Surveys were done both before and after to ensure that Customers felt supported in the same way and didn't feel like they had something taken away from them. While a few individuals did complain about the new set-up, the overall sentiment from Customers was that they were getting the same level of support and value from the team. The business, however, was spending much less time supporting the group than before.

Ultimately, we realigned the system to meet both halves of the newly defined desired outcomes and improved its efficiency by reducing the time employees spent on manual work within the system. This would free the staff to focus on more activities that would generate additional revenue without detracting from the value provided to Customers.

CLIENT ONBOARDING

Another area where we made big changes was in the several weeks of Client onboarding. Like managing the Facebook group, there was an over-emphasis on personal fulfillment through teaching the tools and techniques. Nobody was looking out for a way of doing it that allowed the business to be profitable.

We adjusted the desired outcome to include a statement related to profitability in addition to educating Customers on tools and techniques. In similar fashion to the adjustments we made for the Facebook group, we started attacking the process of onboarding new Clients. We realized that staff could not continue to put in the same amount of time if the system was to meet its defined outcomes. The amount of time spent by staff doing manual tasks, chasing down homework assignments, and generally supporting the system was excessive.

We did a more thorough analysis here on the inputs and process steps of the onboarding process. Understanding the flow from week to week and what was expected of these new Customers was important for us to redefine how the system could work, provide the same amount of value, and take much less time for manual work.

We tackled the homework problem first. Using Google Forms, Google Sheets, Zapier, and their email application, we were able to create an automated system that allowed people to directly submit their homework assignments via electronic form. (Previously, it was submitted to an email address then manually reviewed for completeness).

At the end of the week, when an assignment was due, the system would check to see if the Customer had submitted their homework. If the Customer hadn't, the system would automatically email and ask them some basic questions to understand if they needed additional support or just more time. By eliminating the extra work around managing homework, the staff were able to claw back 20+ hours of manual work per week.

Another part of the onboarding that we ended up adjusting was the interviewing that happened at the end of the process. Originally, the founder interviewed every single person coming out of the onboarding. This was a two-part process where he first did an assessment to see if the individual was ready to test out and then, assuming they were ready, actually performed the interview process to "graduate" them.

While this was a noble goal and provided good feelings to Customers and good insights to the founder, it wasn't a sustainable practice if the company was to grow. Not only did it consume many hours a week of the founder's time and couldn't be done if the business grew any faster, but it also meant that the founder wasn't working on other tasks that would have been more profitable to the business.

The first thing we did was to automate the assessment. Because there was a fixed set of questions and the answers were straightforward, it was simple to build this into another Google Form and have his Customers respond to the form with their answers. Those answers were then scored and given a pass or fail without anyone having to do anything manually.

The other thing we did was to train other staff members on how to perform the final testing interview. This allowed us to free up some of the founder's time so that he could concentrate more on business and product development.

Another improvement that helped a number of the systems was to add a CRM application. At the start of us working together, information was mostly kept an employees' heads, with some maintained in different Google spreadsheets. This created regular confusion and problems for the team because there was no comprehensive view of Customers and their interactions with staff.

It was hard for any individual staff member to help any particular Customer without talking to everyone first to understand who had talked with the Customer and how the conversations went.

By adding a CRM application, we were able to reduce the number of errors committed by staff, reduce the time spent trying to compare notes on specific Customers, and increased the staff's overall knowledge of each Customer, giving the Customers better experiences.

DEVELOPING SCALABLE PRODUCTS

The third area where we made major changes was in the realm of product development. At the time I started working with this company, they spent no time thinking about how to evolve their current products or how to develop new ones. Knowing that the business was having challenges trying to scale, new feature and product development needed to be digitally focused so that we could increase revenue without putting more burden on the staff or needing to hire new people.

One of the areas where I immediately challenged the founder to think differently was on how he was using and managing events. He was making no net income from events and only charged just to cover his base costs. His events were well attended, and it was obvious from his community that they highly enjoyed these events and got significant value from them. While he was looking at these events as a way to find new Customers, I challenged him to think about how he could use events to actually generate meaningful revenue and value for his Clients.

We didn't get overly caught up in defining a complicated product development system in the short-term. We agreed that there needed to be some time and energy put into product development and pretty much left it at that. There was no new software added, no new process built, and no new systems defined, other than to say he should allocate time each week thinking about new features and new products.

What came out of his thinking over the span of a few weeks was a redefined focus on events. Not just small events that ran a couple of hours on a weekend but large-scale, week-long destination events. He went from planning two-hour events at a local low-cost hotel to five or six-day events at exotic locations. He went from selling tickets at $40 apiece to selling hotel stays for $3,500 apiece. While he can't run these very often and they take much more energy to plan and execute, the new revenue he is generating from these events has had a meaningful improvement in his business.

The few events he has run at this much higher rate so far have all sold out within a few weeks of opening and he continues to plan new large-scale events a few times a year.

In addition to these, he's been able to run a few local weekend events that are a couple of days long and charge enough money to make them profitable. With a new focus on events, he has been able to add significant revenue to his business without needing to make huge changes.

MANAGING CHANGE

Throughout these changes, the founder has done an excellent job maintaining and executing a change management plan which includes regular communication with his staff and Customers about what's happening in the business. He regularly solicits feedback from both and incorporates that into his thinking about the changes he's making.

This has helped them avoid pitfalls of making changes that would scare Customers away or cause problems with his staff. In full disclosure, it hasn't been all roses. He did have to dismiss a staff member after he continued to push back and not participate in changes happening in the business. This is something that can and will happen, but the efforts he's made to keep impacted parties informed of changes well before they happen has helped him to reduce the impact everyone feels.

We also did some light work with metrics across many of these systems. In this case, there was no heavy work here or major changes or complicated systems put in to track metrics in the health of the business. But through the work that we did, we added some lightweight metrics and tools that would enable the business to understand system health.

As part of the new CRM system, a few report views were made to show how Customers move in and out of the business. The founder now knows how to run and analyze his own time study and does that from time to time to check how employees are spending their time. He can also now survey employees or Customers at will, getting an understanding of how attitudes are shifting towards his business. Nothing major, but just enough awareness to be able to see shifts in system health and be able to respond accordingly.

In summary, this business was able to take the principles of this book, and, with my guidance, put into practice new techniques over a six-month period that allowed them to triple their income while reducing their costs. While I was working with them directly, there is nothing I did with them that isn't explained in this book.

You too can have similar results by putting into practice the things that you've read and don't hesitate to reach out if you have questions.

THE SOLO ENTREPRENEUR WORKING TO BUILD HIS NEW BUSINESS

I WORKED with an entrepreneur who was trying to build a fitness-based business alone. He worked as a personal trainer and was trying to figure out how to start his own company in the fitness industry. He had the concept of a training program to get middle-aged dads into better shape but had yet to really start anything other than idea generation.

START AT THE END

We defined the desired outcomes of his business, starting with his desired ultimate outcomes. He was really after financial stability and personal freedom. He was tired of working long hours in the gym and the need to be around to support his Clients every day of the week.

Because he was just starting out, he had no real systems to speak of. He had an idea and a desire – and that was about it. But the outcome optimization approach still worked and provided him with significant value, even though we were looking at building systems from scratch and not evaluating existing systems. After defining his desired ultimate outcomes, we started to outline the basic systems he would need in place in order to have a real business. When just starting out, this doesn't have to be fancy or complicated.

DEFINING NEEDED SYSTEMS

We talked through the sales cycle, splitting it out into a traffic system and a lead/closing system that would help him also get new Customers signed up for his program. We identified some desired outcomes for both the traffic system and the lead/closing system. For the traffic system, the outcome he wanted was to have just the right amount of leads to fill his course every two months. He further defined filling his course as needing 20 people to sign up. This became part of the desired outcome of his lead/closing system. In addition to having 20 people sign up every two months, he further defined the desired outcome of the lead/closing system as providing expectations and the right education to newly signed Clients, so they were prepared on day one to get to work.

He worked to define and build the artifacts needed to educate a Client so they would be prepared on that first day. These became inputs into his system to create the output of a well-educated Customer.

We also spent some time defining the tactics he would use to generate traffic as part of his traffic system. He picked a combination of paid and organic strategies that would generate interest in him as a trainer and his program targeted to dads. Not only did we define the tactics, but we also defined the steps he would use to regularly test and run different ads on different platforms. We also defined the steps he would use to create regular content that could drive organic traffic to his program.

Lastly, we discussed a referral program which would be the third way to generate traffic and potential Customers. We identified the process that Customers would go through to refer somebody, as well as the process he would need to follow in order to fulfil those referrals. Because he was just starting out, we were able to design this as a very low-tech solution that required no software. It meant that he would be doing manual work, but the costs would be limited to just his time.

For all these systems, we identified the metrics that would allow us to understand and manage the health of the systems. For the traffic system, he would track his ad spend and click-through rates, as well as website referrals from his organic content. For his lead/closing system, he would track leads coming into the system and conversion of those leads to sales. For the referral system, he would track the referring Customer and the name of the person referred. He could then later identify who signed up from a referral and who didn't.

THINKING THROUGH PRODUCT DE-VELOPMENT

We also spent some time talking about how he was going to develop the course he wanted to build. This included covering what types of materials he would want available for those in his class, how he would deliver information (video, email, lives, etc.), and what applications he would use to deliver the content.

He already had an outline of how the four-week course would go, so this was just a matter of identifying the different pieces and how he planned on creating them. We didn't get into a heavy discussion on building a product development system, but he took that away as homework to do once he had a couple of rounds of his course completed.

He also had already researched applications he could use to deliver the course content and had chosen a purpose-built application, specific to delivering personal training courses. It was the best option since it was catered towards personal training and gave him functionality specific to his industry.

As we designed these new systems, we also aligned the inputs, process steps, and outputs to the desired outcomes of the individual systems, as well as the overall business. By keeping these things in mind, we were able to define systems that were efficient and productive from the start. Every step we added to our process moved us towards the desired outcomes that had been defined.

CHANGE MANAGEMENT LIGHT

Because this was a new business, there wasn't much to do in the way of change management. However, we took some time to establish some baseline metrics that would show the overall health of each system.

Some of these metrics were the standard numbers associated with running online advertisements, as well as standard sales conversion and cost-per-Customer acquisition metrics. Another metric we defined was to capture the readiness of new Clients each time a new round of his course started. He identified a quick and dirty scale he could use to give each Client a one to ten rating of how prepared they were on the first day and tracked that in a Google Sheet.

This new business is still in development at the time of writing, so the actual results remain to be seen. But this gives you an idea of how the framework covered in this book can apply to a brand-new business that has zero systems and processes.

The principles remain the same and by planning ahead, you can build your systems to be effective, efficient and productive from the get-go.

THE LARGE CORPORATION

A LARGE corporation brought me in because they were having major problems with their core systems. These problems manifested as invoicing issues that showed up on an accounting audit – and they were not pretty. In short, the company had incorrectly invoiced several Customers. At the beginning of the project, the scope of the problem wasn't clearly understood, but later analysis would show the company under-billed Clients by more than $3million over a 12-month period.

In addition, they also over-billed some Clients by $1.5million over the same period. Most of the $3million not collected had to be written off while the $1.5million was refunded to those Customers.

Overall, that was a $4.5million hit to their bottom line.

DEFINING SYSTEM SCOPE

Let's go back to the beginning of the problem. As I mentioned, it was discovered in an audit that several invoices had been sent out with incorrect bill rates. As the auditors pulled new invoices to check, they continued to find errors in what was billed. The company decided they had to do something to figure out what was going on – in other words, why they weren't achieving the desired outcome of accurate invoices.

I was brought in and given the charge to look at the company's entire systems and processes from the moment a person was identified as a possible lead to the time services were delivered, final bills were paid, and projects were closed. For a company of 400 employees generating more than $100million a year, this was a big initiative.

ADJUSTING THE APPROACH

Because of the size of this issue, I approached it a little bit differently. I started by breaking out the teams, then identifying the key stakeholders and subject matter experts I would need to work with to understand the systems within each team. Knowing that this project would span multiple teams and multiple key executives, I needed to understand early on who I would need to talk to and who I required to be involved for the project to be successful.

This also posed challenges from the perspective that in defining desired outcomes, you're not just working with one founder. Instead, you're working with different teams and department heads that quite possibly have different objectives and don't necessarily see eye to eye on what their team is doing.

As such, I started my change management plan immediately. Part of identifying the teams and systems I would need to work with, as well as the subject matter experts, was so that I could begin change management practices right away. It was no secret to anybody in the company that I was working on an initiative that would probably impact their area.

I also began building relationships with people across these different teams so that when it came time for me to work with them individually, they would know a little bit about who I was and what I was doing. This allowed me to set things up so that I could start involving people in change early in the process, taking feedback and input from those on the ground doing the work.

What I didn't need to do in this case was to try and define ultimate outcomes. The company wanted to make money and nothing else really mattered. They weren't trying to make anybody feel better and, as a corporation, free time or freedom were not relevant outcomes. With the understanding that anything and everything should be maximizing the ultimate outcome of money, I went to work with the individual teams to define their desired outcomes.

WORKING BACKWARD TO GO FOR-WARD

Starting at the end and working backward, I began working with the accounting team to define their systems for invoicing and the outcomes that they wanted to achieve from that system. The accounting team wanted nothing more than to provide the right invoices to the right Clients at the right time. We didn't dive into other accounting topics such as revenue recognition or financial analysis as everything except invoicing was identified as out of scope for my project.

With the desired outcomes identified, we began to document the process. Because we were looking at so many processes and so many systems, I took the approach of using a more formal strategy to do process documentation. This included creating swimlane diagrams and a SIPOC for every process I was looking at. Remember, a SIPOC is a Six Sigma tool used to document the Suppliers, Inputs, Process steps, Outputs, and Customers of a system. It would be needed to allow us to draw correlations between the different attributes so that I could iden-tify what to fix to get alternative outcomes.

After finishing with the accounting team, I continued to work backward and moved to the team responsible for delivering service to the Cus-tomer. This team delivered the service/product to the Customer, but was also responsible for indicating to accounting that they should start the invoicing process.

In a similar fashion to the accounting team, I worked with the service delivery team to identify which systems they used to execute on their body of work. I documented these systems with swimlane diagrams and SIPOCs, just like I did the accounting team.

The service delivery team called out three specific systems. System one covered how they onboarded new projects. System two covered how they delivered to service over the life of a contract. System three cov-ered how they closed a project down once a contract was over. We also identified the desired outcomes of each of the systems.

After finishing with the service delivery team, I next moved to the procurement and asset management teams. These two teams were responsible for managing the assets needed to deliver on a contract, which often included computers, monitors, phone systems, and other related technology.

Using the swimlane diagram and SIPOC approach, I first outlined the asset management system. This included checking for assets we already had that were not currently deployed on projects and comparing that to the list of needed equipment for each new project. If assets did not exist or were deployed on other projects, the asset management team would communicate those missing assets to the procurement team. The procurement team then had a system for going out and acquiring new assets. Once new assets were acquired, there was another system owned by the asset management team to bring those new assets into the company and ensure they got labeled and entered onto a tracking application.

Next on my list, I worked with the sales team to understand their system for kicking off newly won business. The sales team was responsible for pushing the button on the system that started the official process for a new delivery project for a Customer. We documented their process and defined their desired outcomes.

Before the sales team officially kicked off any new project, all contracts were reviewed by our contracts team. Their piece of the puzzle was quite simple as they had a system to review the paper contracts, looking for legal issues or inconsistencies with master service agreements with Customers. Draft contracts came in and executed contracts went out.

At this point, I came back to the service delivery team as they owned a piece in the middle of the sales processes. The service delivery team was responsible for working with the sales team to ensure that projects were scoped correctly and had the right roles and equipment priced in the contract to be able to deliver to the Customer.

Once I finished with the service delivery team (again), I went back to the sales team for the final piece of the overall process. This covered the timeline from sales identifying a potential lead to the time that contract negotiations began and the service delivery team was invited to help scope the project.

DOCUMENTING WITH TOOLS

I followed my same method of documenting the systems with the swimlane diagram and a SIPOC for each system. In the first part of the sales process, the sales team identified three systems. One for generating new contacts and another for nurturing those contacts into qualified leads. The third took those qualified leads and converted them into potential sales that kicked off the scoping system with the service delivery team. After defining the desired outcomes and the system attributes, we finally had a first look at the end-to-end process – starting with the initial contact by our sales team and through the delivery of the project to accounting finishing the billing and closing the engagement.

We could now start working on aligning desired outcomes of these systems across the different teams…almost.

While they did not run a system as part of this end-to-end process, I also worked with the IT team to understand their involvement and their systems for maintaining software used throughout the process.

The company had a project management application developed in-house and that was used to run the end-to-end process. The sales team started using this application to track and manage leads. The asset management and sales teams used this system to track their assets and assign assets to projects. The service delivery team used the system to track project hours and contract fulfillment. The accounting team used the same system to create invoices and send them to the Customers.

I needed to work with the IT team because they carried out all the tasks needed to make any changes to the application. In that regard, they were a stakeholder and subject matter expert. They also understood what was happening under the hood of the application, so they were a resource for helping to identify problems and inefficiencies in the processes and data flows.

At this point, I had talked to everyone involved and we were ready to move on to getting alignment of outcomes. We had six different teams and 13 different systems involved in this process. Aligning on outcomes would be challenging to say the least.

OUTCOME ALIGNMENT

One of the challenges when aligning desired system outcomes across multiple teams is that each team is often only interested in their own problems and needs. Even when companies have friendly, cooperative environments, this can prove to be challenging. This was no different.

For example, the asset management team had the desired outcome of getting all assets into their asset management system before they were deployed. While this was a good outcome for them, sometimes it conflicted with what the service delivery team wanted. Some projects were short on time and service delivery wanted assets deployed immediately without having to wait for the asset management team to finish their intake process of new assets.

These types of smaller-scale conflicts existed at every hand-off between teams and had to be resolved in a way that made both teams feel good about the desired outcomes of each of the systems, while keeping in mind the ultimate outcome of making as much money as possible.

One of the biggest conflicts in defining outcomes came with the sales systems. As part of their process in winning and kicking off new projects, the sales team was responsible for entering in bill rates that were later used in the invoicing process. It was identified early on that this was a likely source for the company's invoicing issues, so it was a hot topic from the beginning.

Sales already didn't like that they had to do data entry work to get bill rates into the application, but there was nobody else in the company who was going to do it. The contracts team was too small to do their regular workload plus data entry. The service delivery team refused to do it and there was really no other option. It had been the sales team's job since the beginning of the company and it really had no other home.

Accounting wanted to modify the desired outcomes of the upfront sales systems to include language on the accuracy and timeliness of bill rate entry. While the sales team didn't disagree that this was a good outcome, the language used to define the desired outcomes of the sales systems left much to interpretation and significant wiggle room for them to deny accountability if problems continue to happen.

In an effort to make progress, I left the soft language in and moved on to the next steps in my process.

At this point, we had well-defined processes and systems from start to finish and generally aligned desired outcomes for the complete process. We had a better understanding of the software and some of its shortcomings, and we were ready to start prioritizing where we wanted to focus our improvement efforts.

USING TOOLS TO IMPROVE

One of the tools we used at this point to start to get to the root cause of the invoicing problem was the five whys.

Why are the invoices incorrect? Because the bill rates are incorrect.

Why are the bill rates incorrect? Because they were entered into the system incorrectly.

Why are they entered into the system incorrectly? Because the sales team enters the bill rates and they are less diligent about data entry and pressured to move on quickly to the next sale.

Why does the sales team enter the bill rates? Because there is no one else to enter them.

I used another Six Sigma tool known as the FMEA (Failure Modes and Effects Analysis) to do prioritization of the work on the 13 different systems. The FMEA is a tool that looks at the possible system or process failures, the frequency of those failures, the pain those failures cause, and the difficulty to remedy the failures when they happen. It then calculates a score based on these variables that tells you the inputs and outputs you should focus on to optimize your systems.

Note that properly completing an FMEA, especially for a process this large, is a very time-consuming effort that produces results that are arguably not worth the effort. In my career, I can't say that I've ever gotten significantly different results from using an FMEA over having a conversation with the people involved in the system about where failures happen and how the system should be improved.

The only reason I did it in this case was because the company requested it as a more scientific approach to identifying where the focus would be on fixing the problems.

Based on the completion of the FMEA, we now had a prioritized list of problems to fix. At the top of the list was the process in the sales system to enter bill rates into our project management application. Specific to improving the invoicing, there were also some minor improvements to make in the accounting systems to ensure accurate and timely invoicing. As this project was focused on improving the invoicing with some sense of urgency, we limited the scope at this point to only working on problems that would improve the accuracy of the invoicing.

RECOMMENDATIONS AND CHANGES

From completing the five whys exercise and reinforcing the root of the problem with the FMEA, I recommended that the company establish a new admin team to do the data entry on behalf of the sales team.

This team would focus solely on entering contract data, including the bill rates, into the project management software. These would be people hired because of their attention to detail and they would not be part of the sales team, being rushed off to try and make more sales.

With a tentative approval to build this new team, I set out to rebuild the processes and systems in a way that was more efficient, productive, and effective.

The first thing I did was to redefine desired outcomes assuming this new team was in place. It meant that the sales team just cared about making the sale and getting the paperwork to this new team. The new team was then responsible for the next system in the process with the desired outcome that aligned with the contracts and accounting teams' desires to have more accountability on the people entering the data.

With new outcomes defined and aligned, I began to define the new processes within each system. Again, I was only focused on areas that would improve Customer invoicing. While this focus was limited, there were still changes to many of the systems in order to make the new team functional and create the proper workflow through the systems.

Starting from the beginning, I worked through the sales processes, eliminating, consolidating, and automating where I could. I already had all the documentation from the initial exercises in creating swimlanes and SIPOCs for each of the systems. I was able to evaluate each step in the process, eliminating those that didn't add value and were no longer necessary. I consolidated workflows around this new team and the work that they would be able to accomplish. After that, I automated everything I could to remove the possibility of human error.

As the changes that would actually occur became clearer, I turned up my change management activities. When contemplating changes to a specific team's system, I would involve that team in the discussion. I brought with me the data, analysis, and thinking that had been done in a certain area and used that to brainstorm with each group about changes that would impact them. In this manner, they all felt like the changes were partly their ideas and not just mine. It's much easier to change when you're changing because you want to and not because somebody else told you to.

I also began communicating to the broader group about changes happening across the entire system so that people were brought along for the journey, understood some of the thinking that went into the changes that were happening, and wouldn't be surprised later on when the software or process was actually changed.

I was also heavily involved with the IT team at this point, working through how the applications needed to change in order to support the new processes and systems. Since the project management tool was all custom code, this was a large effort.

The company was not interested in developing new metrics to track and manage to understand the health of these systems. The decision was made that the reporting already in the system was "good enough" and that no additional time or money should be spent improving the reporting. Despite this, there was a new process added within the accounting team to spot check more invoices each month to ensure accuracy. The accounting team also worked closely with the new team that had been established to do the data entry to ensure that every contract was entered completely and that any nuances specific to billing were clearly called out.

FINAL RESULTS

In summary, this was a six-month project designed to reduce invoicing problems for a company that had lost $3million and had to give another $1.5million back to Customers as refunds because of invoicing problems over a 12-month period.

In the 12 months after the project, a later audit showed less than $30,000 of invoice discrepancies.

Just that alone improved the company's bottom line by $3million, not even considering efficiency improvements made to eliminate waste and automate other parts of the overall process.

The cost of the new team was less than $300,000 per year. And this new team saved the sales team 8,600 hours per year of administrative work, leaving them that time to focus on more sales. The company saved millions and made millions more by optimizing for outcomes.

THE MANUFACTURER

A MANUFACTURING company brought me in to help with a specific system in their business — they wanted to improve the way they developed new products. This company manufactured electronics used in the construction industry. They had a good product and had been in business for many years but had little visibility into recent trends on how their Customers were using their products. That meant they played a bit of a guessing game while trying to develop new features they thought Customers would be interested in.

What they realized is that sometimes this works and sometimes it doesn't. However, they also knew they could take a more scientific approach and get it right more often than not. Unsure of the best way to approach this challenge, they reached out to me.

FOCUSING STRAIGHTAWAY ON A SPECIFIC SYSTEM

The first thing I did was to look at how they were developing products. This included understanding how they identified and prioritized new features to build into existing products and how they decided to build an entirely new product.

I also worked with the executive leadership team to define their desired outcomes for a product development system. This was defined as "designing and building cutting-edge technology that is the right technology for the job, is easy to use, and makes construction sites safer".

With this newly defined desired outcome, we worked backward to figure out how we would need to redesign the system. We defined the outputs needed to achieve the desired outcome. To make sure it was the right technology for the job, we would need to design products that weren't too little or too much. To make sure the products were easy to use, we would need logical and clean user interfaces that could be navigated while someone was wearing gloves. To build a product that made construction sites safer, we would need to understand current safety challenges and build features into the product that helped address those challenges.

With a better understanding of the outputs needed to achieve the desired outcome, we could then identify inputs needed to make those outputs a reality. To know if the product was too much or too little, we would need real-world data on how the equipment was being used at construction sites. We would need a profile of the construction sites to understand the environment, what work was being done, and other related information.

For ease of use, we would need a better understanding of the end-users' process and how they were using the equipment. We would also need their feedback to understand what was confusing to them and where they might be getting stuck using the equipment.

From a safety perspective, we needed insights into regular construction site mishaps. By understanding the safety problems that were happening at these sites, we could then consider features and functionality to reduce these mishaps occurring.

HOW TO GET THE INPUTS

At this point, we had established the inputs needed to create the outputs necessary to generate the outcomes the business wanted. The next step was to identify how we would get the inputs and what the process would be to turn those inputs into the outputs.

The company had field staff that regularly visited Customers' construction sites and these field employees were a vital source of information about what was happening day to day. The challenge the company faced was that the information rarely left the minds of the field staff and there were no mechanisms in place to capture and analyze the things they were learning on a daily basis.

I very quickly set up the tools to allow field staff to report on their daily visits to construction sites. While we could have spent months building fancy technology to do this, I opted for a spreadsheet set up in a shared location that took a couple hours to set up. Even though the company had the money to invest in a more elegant solution, using the spreadsheet allowed us to start collecting data right away and save the company money in the short term. The added benefit to this approach was that we were able to make tweaks over the following weeks to improve our system and all it took was modifying a spreadsheet.

In addition to recording construction site information, the field staff were also asked to do a deep dive on one site per quarter. This entailed writing a detailed report of everything observed on a single construction site from the start to end of a project (most projects were started and completed in one to three days). These detailed reports helped paint a better picture not only of the construction site environment, but also how Customers were using the equipment and what problems they were running into with the product's usability. Additionally, these reports were used to identify safety issues at the construction sites.

Another team identified as having regular contact with Customers and able to provide good information for product features was the product support team. This was a team that provided phone and email support for end-users in the field. They routinely worked with Customers having problems with the equipment and understood the end-users better than anybody else in the company.

Like the field staff, the product support team had a wealth of knowledge that was all captured in individuals' heads. Each of the support staff had many conversations every day with end-users that were actively using the equipment on construction sites.

To harness this team, their experience, and their regular interactions with end-users, we also set up a tracking system that allowed the team to record details of their conversations. Again, we took the scrappy approach of building a tracking tool in a spreadsheet where we could then consolidate information from across the team and start to analyze the data. Each call or email was recorded and details logged about the construction site, the work being done with the equipment, and any problems the end-users experienced.

Both the field staff and product support teams were trained to adjust their regular conversations to talk more about safety concerns at the construction sites. This allowed the company to augment their information with potential safety hazards and problem solve on what features could be added to help alleviate some of the safety issues.

BRINGING IT ALL TOGETHER

With systems in place to gather the inputs, consolidate, and analyze them, we then worked with the organization to establish how they would use this new information to build features into their products.

The company had an engineering team that was responsible for the actual product development. I worked with the engineering director to build a process for scoring the priority of Customer problems and related features. As we consolidated and analyzed data from Customers, the engineering team went through and defined possible solutions with the level of effort needed to complete each solution. The information was then pushed into the scoring system which identified the top priorities based on the frequency of problem, the pain level it created, and level of effort to fix the problem.

While it's difficult to say exactly which of the company's results from the following years were related specifically to this work, the releases after the company's product development system was optimized have been the best and most well-received in many years.

By adapting their product development system to be more focused on Customer feedback, the company has been able to right-size the cost of their equipment relative to the work Customers are using it for, as well as being able to add new features that are loved by its Customers.

GLOSSARY

Change Management
The discipline of dealing with adjustments that happen in business. Change management is about identifying people that are impacted by change, then managing the work needed to make the change happen and become the new normal.

CRM
Customer Relationship Management software. A CRM is used by businesses to track key Customer information and record interactions between the Customer and the company.

Desired Outcomes
The expected results of a system.

Downstream
In the world of processes and systems, each step in the process/system has a relationship to other process steps that is said to be "upstream" or "downstream." Downstream process steps happen AFTER the step they are being compared to (e.g. step 4 is downstream from step 1).

This is an important designation because downstream problems are often caused by problems happening further upstream in the process. Another way to think of this is fixing upstream process steps can often resolve downstream problems.

Effectiveness
A measure of how well an output of a system meets the intended purpose of the output.

Effectiveness can also refer to a measure of how well a system is delivering its desired outcomes.

Efficiency
A ratio of inputs, outputs, and time to produce outputs in a system. Efficiency increases under the following conditions:
- Producing more outputs with the same inputs.
- Producing the same outputs with fewer inputs.
- Producing the same outputs with the same inputs in shorter time.

Five Pillars
There are five main areas or "pillars" in any business.

- Sales Cycle – how a business generates traffic and converts that traffic to sales.
- Product Cycle – how a business builds and refines its products.
- Operations – the collection of administrative systems that help the business function.
- People Management – the systems that help a company hire, inspire, rewire, and retire employees.
- Culture – a collection of artifacts, policies, guidelines, and beliefs that defines how employees of a business will operate.

Five Whys
A method of doing root cause analysis. For any situation, the user asks themselves "why does this happen?". The user continues to ask "why?" until they are satisfied that they have identified the root cause of the issue they are trying to solve. Five is not an exact number to always hit when using this method of analysis.

Why does A happen? Because B happens.

Why does B happen? Because C happens.

Why does C happen? And so on.

FMEA
A tool used to identify potential failures in a system. FMEA is an acronym that stands for Failure Modes and Effects Analysis. The user first documents how a process step might fail and then assesses the frequency, impact, and detectability of said failure.

The tool then produces out a score that can be used to stack rank all failures to identify which are bigger problems.

Input
One of the key system attributes, an input is some resource that is consumed by a system. Often times an input for a specific process step is an output of a previous step.

Metric
One of the key system attributes, a metric is a single point of data that measures outcomes, outputs, process throughput, inputs, etc. specific to running your business. Metrics should be consistently measurable and easy to collect.

Outcome Optimization Framework
The tools, mental models, and mindset needed to think about your business in systems and to optimize the systems within the business to get better outcomes.

Output
One of the key system attributes, an output is the thing or things produced by a process step in a system. Outputs often become inputs to steps later in the system or become inputs to another system.

Process Narrative
A written description of how a process flows. The description is usually a numbered, bulleted list of steps in the order in which they are performed.

Process Step
One of the key system attributes, process steps are the actions that are performed by a person or technology with a system.

Productivity
The measure of outputs from a system.

SIPOC
A tool used to document systems. SIPOC is an acronym which stands for Supplier, Input, Process step, Output, Customer. To use a SIPOC, each process step in the system is first documented. Then, for each step,

the inputs required to complete that step, as well as the supplier of those inputs, are identified. Lastly, the outputs of the step are defined as well as the Customer of those outputs.

Six Sigma
A process improvement methodology used by corporations across the world. Six Sigma has been lauded by many as a scientific way to systematically make a company more effective by reducing "defects" in systems. It has a number of critics, too, who claim it stifles innovation and hurts companies more than it helps.

Swimlane Diagram
A method of documenting a process which produces a diagram that looks like a large swimming pool with lanes. Each lane represents a "doer" in the process and is filled with the tasks the doer is responsible for completing.

System
Often thought of incorrectly as software, a system is a collection of people, processes, and/or technology that have a purpose to achieve one or more desired outcomes. A system will always have process steps and with include either people, technology, or both.

System Attributes
The pieces that make up a system. System attributes include inputs, process steps, outputs, metrics, and desired outcomes.

Systems Thinking
A method of thinking about your business (or anything else that has a purpose of doing work) in a systematized manner. Smaller systems make larger systems that eventually comprise the whole of your business. These systems have attributes and characteristics that allow you to understand a common set of tools and methods to improve a system and apply those tools and methods to any part of your business.

Ultimate Outcomes
Commonly referred to as the "Big Y" (or the "Big Why"), ultimate outcomes define the reason an entrepreneur is in business. As part of the

Outcome Optimization Framework, there are three answers to this question:

- Money.
- Time/Freedom.
- Personal Fulfillment.

Upstream

In the world of processes and systems, each step in the process/system has a relationship to other process steps that is said to be "upstream" or "downstream". Upstream process steps happen BEFORE the step they are being compared to (e.g. step 1 is upstream from step 4).

This is an important designation because downstream problems are oftentimes caused by problems happening further upstream in the process. Another way to think of this is fixing upstream process steps can often resolve downstream problems.

Printed in Great Britain
by Amazon